CURING
THE HEART

Dr. Howard Eyrich serves on the Pastoral Staff at Briarwood Presbyterian Church. He has not only developed, but put into practice, the model of Biblical Counseling which is developed for you in this book. Our Lord has used him successively to minister to many people in our congregation and community, to train others and to multiply biblical counseling through the transferable model that you will find on the following pages. The blessing of this ministry is evident, not only in the lives of the people that it touches, but also in the many lay people that he has trained to assist in the counseling ministry at Briarwood.

Dr. Harry L. Reeder, III, Sr. Pastor, Briarwood Presbyterian Church Birmingham, Alabama

Curing the Heart: A Model for Biblical Counseling joins the still small literature of the growing Biblical Counseling movement. From the authors' broad experience it uniquely and most importantly provides actual guidance for the Christian who is called to counsel. This guidance is born of the conviction that the work of Christ and Scripture are sufficient to godly change. This is an important contribution and should be read and studied accordingly.

Gary Almy, M.D., Author, *How Christian is Christian Counseling?*

Eyrich and Hines' new *Curing the Heart: A Model for Biblical Counseling* is outstanding!
Their multidimensional approach focuses on several facets of counseling that help the counselor be fully equipped to deal with every kind of problem situation. Get one for yourself and one for everyone you know who is interested in counseling people God's way.

Dr. Ed Hindson, Assistant Chancellor, Liberty University, Lynchburg, Virginia

As a student pastor, the *Curing the Heart* model of Biblical counseling changed the course of my ministry. It equipped me with the biblical knowledge and tools to minister to those in distress, debt and discontent.

Rev. John Battle, Alpine, Alabama

CURING THE HEART

A MODEL FOR BIBLICAL COUNSELING

HOWARD EYRICH

&

WILLIAM HINES

MENTOR

ISBN 1-85792-722-2

© Copyright Howard A. Eyrich and William L. Hines 2002

Published in 2002
by
Christian Focus Publications, Ltd
Geanies House, Fearn, Tain,
Ross-shire, IV20 1TW, UK.

www.christianfocus.com

Printed and bound by
JW Arrowsmith, Bristol

Cover Design by Alister MacInnes

CONTENTS

DEDICATION

We would like to dedicate this book to our students and counselees. They have blessed us in our interchanges with them. Our students have been our encouragement as they have absorbed the content we have taught and then multiplied our efforts as they have taught and counseled others. Our counselees have encouraged us in two ways. First, by the change in their lives that has glorified God and brought them peace. Second, by causing us to constantly re-examine our own lives before God as we expose them to the Word of God. May the reading and use of this book bring the same blessings to you as you reach out to teach and counsel others.

ACKNOWLEDGMENTS

I would like to thank Dr. Jay Adams and Dr. John Bettler for their mentorship as well as the opportunity to teach and counsel at the Christian Counseling and Educational Foundation for some five years in the 1970s. It was there that my approach to teaching Biblical Counseling was hammered out on the anvils of counseling and teaching. I would also like to acknowledge the many pastors and lay people who were my students during those years. The Supper Seminar in which cases were discussed and critiqued was an invaluable learning module. Since those days there have been five key students who have been "iron sharpening iron" to me. They are Dr. Andrew Boswell, Rev. Lou Priolo, Judy Dabler, and Micky and Susan Roper. In His grace, the Lord placed these people in my life to teach, rebuke, correct and sometimes force me to develop in training in righteousness. To God be the glory!

Howard Eyrich

I am indebted to many for their mentoring of me through the years. Dr. Howard Eyrich has not only allowed me to know him as a Mentor and colleague but as a friend. My brother and fellow counselor, Mark Hines, first opened up the Scriptures to me through his changed life and prayerful dedication to not leaving me behind in the great adventure of knowing Christ. Francis Schaeffer taught me to think within a biblical framework, and S. Lewis Johnson and Louis Berkhof helped me learn to order my thinking theologically. My wife, Kathy, and children, Michelle, Kristin, Austin, Elise and Anna, live within the laboratory of life with me in such a way as to challenge me to live what I teach and to see the reality of God's mercy when I fail to do so. My fellow Board members at the International Association of Biblical Counselors are a source of encouragement through their unwavering commitment to biblical counseling and Sue Hulett, colleague and friend, provides a constant exhibition of the true heart of a counselor for Christ. Finally, I want to thank Brad and Julie Beauchamp, Steve and Marlene Crist and Bill and Laura Waybourn for continually holding me up in prayer and providing a source of accountability for our ministry. May God be honored!

Bill Hines, Summer 2002

SPECIAL ACKNOWLEDGMENTS

We want to thank the following for their commitment to and help with this project:

Robert Hines and Judy Dabler provided great help by reading the manuscript and making valuable comments as to style and content.

Laura Waybourn worked under a tight schedule to complete the subject index. Elise Hines brings pride to her father's heart by her tireless work on the Scripture index.

Finally, we want to thank Malcolm Maclean and Martin Maclean at Christian Focus Publications for their vision and patience and the whole staff at Christian Focus and Mentor Publications for bringing the project to fruition.

INTRODUCTION

The Puritans used to speak of the curing of souls. They believed that with the Bible rightly applied one could take a person successfully through the process of sanctification in a way that pleases God and brings peace to the soul. This book is dedicated to the idea that the Bible contains all that is needed for life and godliness (2 Peter 1:2-4) and that it is the only rule of faith and obedience. Upon that foundation we have put together a paradigm for thinking through the implications of such a perspective, the people who are qualified to carry on the ministry of counseling and a model for the counseling session. This third aspect of the book deserves some qualification. The model presented is biblical in that each item presented is presented with Scriptural support and an apologetic for its inclusion in the model. We want to stress, however, that it is *a* model. The Bible does not lay out such a precise model and we do not want to give the impression that there is just one way to carry on a counseling session. We have, however, found it invaluable to give our students this model as they begin this fascinating ministry and have found it gives them greater confidence as they have a systematic way of approaching the session and greater patience to allow the counselee's story to unfold.

SECTION ONE

THE NEED FOR A
BIBLICAL APPROACH

CHAPTER 1

WHAT DO THE HEAVENS DECLARE?

If one listens to the voices of popular culture it seems there is a return to spirituality. One popular talk show host talks of getting in touch with your spirit, while another speaks of getting to know God through nature. But is man able to truly know God by getting "in touch" with himself or exploring the wonders of nature?

The various aspects of creation are spoken of in theology as general revelation, that is, the revelation of God in a general way, a way that every human should understand. Dr. B. A. Demerest describes general revelation as:

That divine disclosure to all persons at all times and all places by which one comes to know that God is, and what he is like. While not imparting saving truths such as the Trinity, incarnation, or atonement, general revelation mediates the conviction that God exists and that he is self-sufficient, transcendent, immanent, eternal, powerful, wise, good, and righteous. General, or natural revelation may be divided into two categories: (1) internal, the innate sense of deity and conscience, and (2) external, nature and providential history.[1]

Dr. Wayne Grudem succinctly defines general revelation this way:

The knowledge of God's existence, character, and moral law which comes through creation to all humanity.[2]

---

[1] *Evangelical Dictionary of Theology*, Walter Elwell, ed., Baker Book House, Grand Rapids, MI, 1984.
[2] *Systematic Theology* Wayne Grudem, Zondervan Publishing, Grand Rapids, MI 1994, p.120.

Examples of general revelation

Examples of the workings of general revelation from Scripture include Acts 14:17 where God is said to have given witness of Himself by providing rains and food even to those who have rebelled against Him.

Romans 1:18-21 is often quoted in regard to general revelation since it includes the testimony that God is revealed in His wrath as one who actively punishes the suppression of the truth that He has made evident, and within man as a God who has actually placed the knowledge of Himself within the creature (innate sense), and in history and providence through the display of His power and nature to the extent that man is without excuse.

Following the argument all the way through Romans 1:18-32 the biblical counselor gains much insight pertaining to what happens in the person who rejects God. We see right away that there is no such thing as an isolated sin that only affects the person for the moment, for with each sin comes an active suppression of the knowledge of God by the sinner (vv. 18-19). Since man does, in some sense, know God (v. 21) yet rebels against such knowledge, God's wrath is revealed to the end that the sinner experiences greater hardening of heart and greater conformity to the world system that creates its own gods (which makes man the ultimate authority). This is further accomplished with the approval of the inner man that has become hardened to the true knowledge of God because of his suppression of the truth revealed. The biblical counselor should emphasize that this digression within the human heart often has the approval of the heart of man because man is allowed to believe what he is insistent on believing (see vv. 24, 28, 32).

Psalm 19:1-4 contains another definitive declaration of the general revelation of God:

> The heavens declare the glory of God; and the firmament shows His handiwork. Day unto day utters speech, and night unto night reveals knowledge. There is no speech nor language where their voice is not heard. Their line has gone out through all the earth, and their words to the end of the world.

The creation speaks to us of knowledge of the Creator. It brings a sense of wonder to our hearts yet raises more questions than it answers. For instance, we may realize there must be an intelligent designer behind the design but we don't know His name or whether we can know Him. We may see that He is a Creator given to beauty yet we don't know why the same universe that gives us a beautiful sunrise or cool breeze also brings drought or earthquake. We observe that parts of the creation die or experience pain yet we do not know why.

Responding to general revelation

These and other such questions are responded to in a variety of ways. Some respond by saying God is unknowable. Others believe God is a God of beauty and love yet not able to deal effectively with pain and suffering. Others determine to worship creation itself. It is easy to see how simply observing creation does not give the kind of definition man needs to determine who God is. As R. C. Sproul notes:

> One of the most important advantages the Bible gives us is that it provides information that is not available anywhere else... But with all the skills of knowledge that we have at our disposal in this world, there is no one who can speak to us from a transcendent perspective...

and later:

> ... the world's best geographer cannot show us the way to God, and the world's best psychiatrist cannot give us a final answer to the problem of our guilt.[3]

In the arena of helping people in our present time the argument is the same when we examine the dilemma of hurting people. Disciplines such as psychology, sociology, history and medicine are, at best, able only to make general observations.

---

[3] *Knowing Scripture* by R. C. Sproul, InterVarsity Press, 1977, pp. 23-24.

They cannot answer the *why* of the human condition. For example, modern medicine can tell us that an appendix has burst and must be removed so that the patient will not die but it cannot tell us ultimately why the body deteriorates. Sociology and psychology may observe and catalog human behaviors but they cannot tell us the workings or condition of the human heart out of which such responses flow (Proverbs 4:23; Matthew 12:34; Luke 6:45). When they try to explain the *why* of human behavior their guess is no better than the untrained or unlearned because they are, in the final analysis, simply making observations based on general revelation. This is not to say that their observations are simplistic. At times they are very complex and creative. It is to say, however, that they are limited because they lack the knowledge of what is behind creation and the meaning of life within the creation. Theirs is the same assumption pointed out by theologian Herman Bavinck: "By nature we consider ourselves and our abilities, the world and its treasures, enough for our salvation."[4] For there to be understanding of the creation it must come from the Creator who designed it with purpose. It is He who must tell us what His purpose is if we are to understand. Only the Creator could answer the question posed by the young boy who gazed at the night sky and asked. "Where does space end, and what is on the other side of the end?"

So what do the heavens declare? They declare the wonder of a Creator with great power (Romans 1:18-32). They declare something of the moral law and character of God (Romans 2:14-15) and they also point us to the need for a word from that Creator if we are to know the why – the meaning – of what we are observing. That word must come from the God who transcends His creation because every observer is part of the creation itself and is, therefore, finite and does not have the knowledge necessary to understand and speak to the heart of man.

---

[4] *Our Reasonable Faith* by Herman Bavinck, Baker Book House, 1977, p.61.

CHAPTER 2

THE BIBLE AS THE VOICE OF GOD

The insufficiency of general revelation to speak to the heart of man makes special revelation a necessity. Special revelation consists of God's words addressed to specific people. These words would include the words of the Bible, Old Testament prophets, New Testament apostles, the words spoken at Sinai or those spoken at the baptism of Jesus.[5] Such words are the truthful revelation of God.

When a prophet in the Old Testament spoke for God he had to be one hundred per cent accurate. Such was the case stated in Deuteronomy 18:18-20. In these verses we are told that the true prophet of God will speak the words of God and those who hear the Word will be required to heed those words or face dire consequences.[6]

God's voice is needed because God has dominion
God's voice is needed because as Creator and King over the universe man is subject to Him. In His position as Creator and King, God has dominion over:

• **Creation:** Genesis 1 shows the Creator at work. As Creator He has authority over all He created which includes not only things physical but things immaterial as well as God breathing the breath of life into Adam (Genesis 2:7).

---

[5] See: *Systematic Theology* by Wayne Grudem, Zondervan Publishing, 1994, p. 123.
[6] The implications should be clear for those counselees who claim to have received communication from God or for those who receive the counsel of Scripture and do not heed the counsel.

- **Heaven and Earth:** in Daniel 4:34-35 we find a discourse by the King of Babylon where he recognized that God is the God of heaven and earth. King Nebuchadnezzar makes it clear that the God of heaven does as He wills in the universe and in the lives of people. There is no one who escapes His dominion.

- **Human Authority:** The Apostle Peter tells his readers the same in 1 Peter 2:13-15. Christians are told to honor civil authorities because God is the one who allows the authority to exist. The Apostle Paul makes this clear when he writes, *Let every soul be subject to the governing authorities. For there is no authority except from God, and the authorities that exist are appointed by God* (Romans 13:1).

- **Life and Death:** In Matthew 10:26-31 Jesus makes it clear that God is the God over life and death. In verse 28 He states, *And do not fear those who kill the body but cannot kill the soul. But rather fear Him who is able to destroy both soul and body in hell.* Paul also states his recognition that death no longer has power over the person who belongs to God (1 Corinthians 15:54-58).

- **Morals:** One need look no further than the Ten Commandments (Exodus 20) to recognize that God is the ultimate law giver and states His commands in a way that it is clear that those who follow are subject to blessing from God and those who disobey are subject to His discipline.

In all these areas it is made clear even in the few verses cited that man is responsible to God and is therefore in need of special revelation to know what it is that this God of the universe wants of His creatures.

God's voice is needed because man is in need

Man's need is due to his sinful separation from a holy God. When man sinned in the Garden of Eden he was separated from perfect fellowship with God. This affected man's relationship not only with God but his relationship with himself, with other people, and with nature (Genesis 3:6-24)[7] Since that time man has struggled with sin. God displayed his care and gave a glimpse of the gospel by providing the skins of animals to cover man's nakedness, thus shedding innocent blood to cover man's sin. This example, as with the sacrificial system that followed throughout the Old Testament, was inadequate to do the work which ultimately could only be done by Christ as is argued eloquently in Hebrews 10:1-25.

Man is born into this world as a sinner. His need reaches to his very heart, the core of his being, affecting not simply what he does but who he is. It is the heart of man that is wicked.[8] *The heart is deceitful above all things, And desperately wicked; Who can know it?* (Jeremiah 17:9).[9]

God's voice is needed as an authoritative standard

The Bible is the authoritative voice of God communicated to a people in need of an absolute standard for faith and life. God's Word is authoritative as a word that flows from Himself. The Bible as the Word of God is, therefore, truthful, authoritative, and forever.

• God's word is truth

God's truthfulness means that He is the true God, and that all His knowledge and words are both true and the final standard of truth.[10] What God says is true for He cannot lie (Titus 1:2; Hebrews 6:18). What God says is what He does (Numbers 23:19). There is no disconnect between God's behavior and His statements. What God says is true for mankind is true (2 Samuel 7:28). His specific truth is set forth in His Word for all to heed or ignore, but whether one chooses to ignore it or not, it is no less true. As the Psalmist says, *The entirety of Your word is truth, And every*

---

[7] For a good study on this see *Genesis in Space and Time* by Francis A. Schaeffer, Tyndale House Publishers, 1972, pp. 98-101.

[8] See chapter 5 for more on the heart of man.

[9] For more on the effect of sin on the inner man see verses such as Deuteronomy 18:18-20; Romans 2:14-15; Titus 1:15; Hebrews 10:22; 1 Corinthians 8:10.

[10] *Systematic Theology* by Wayne Grudem, Zondervan Publishing, 1994, p. 195.

one of Your righteous judgments endures forever (Psalm 119:160). And Ezekiel warns that not all who hear the truth will heed the truth: *You shall speak My words to them, whether they hear or whether they refuse, for they are rebellious* (Ezekiel 2:7). But the promise of blessing goes out to all who will hear and heed His Word: *Every word of God is pure; He is a shield to those who put their trust in Him* (Proverbs 30:5). And the warning extends to those who change His Word: *Do not add to His words, Lest He rebuke you, and you be found a liar* (Proverbs 30:6). Counselees who discover the shield of God's Word by faithful obedience will find blessing but those who seek to add to His Word with other traditions or modern theories will not find such blessing. Man is sanctified by the truth which is God's Word: *Sanctify them by Your truth. Your word is truth* (John. 17:17).

• **God's word is authoritative**

The authority of Scripture means that all the words in Scripture are God's Word in such a way that to disbelieve or disobey any word of Scripture is to disbelieve or disobey God.[11]

God's Word was written at God's command and has God's final authority (Exodus 17:14, 34:27; Jeremiah 30:2; Acts 4:24-26; Revelation 1:11-19). It is to Scripture that Bible personalities appealed for authority (Acts 24:14; Romans 3:4; Romans 4:16-24; 1 Corinthians 14:37; 2 Peter 3:16). Those who refuse to obey the words of Scripture are in active disobedience to God (Proverbs 30:5-6; Luke 24:25; John 15:20; 2 Timothy 3:16-17). All authority on earth is only an extension of God's authority and those who exercise authority do so only because God allows them to (Daniel 4:34-35; Romans 13:1; 1 Peter 2:13-16).

• **God's word is forever**

A man who was struggling with sexual temptation told me once that had Jesus lived in our day He would have made different "rules" in the areas in which the man struggled. Many have made such statements presuming that sin today is more difficult to

---

[11] *Systematic Theology* by Wayne Grudem, Zondervan Publishing, 1994, p. 73.

resist than in the times that the Bible was written. The Bible, however, does not give man the option of arbitrarily deciding which parts are valuable for any particular time in history. Consider the following statements of Scripture:

- The grass withers, the flower fades, But the word of our God stands forever (Isaiah 40:8).
- The entirety of Your word is truth, And every one of Your righteous judgments endures forever (Psalm 119:160).
- Do not think that I came to destroy the Law or the Prophets. I did not come to destroy but to fulfill (Matthew 5:17).
- Heaven and earth will pass away, but My words will by no means pass away (Matthew 24:35).
- ... having been born again, not of corruptible seed but incorruptible, through the word of God which lives and abides forever.... (1 Peter 1:23).

When one considers these and similar passages there is a powerful statement that God intends for people of every age to revere His Word and to live by its precepts, as we will discuss in more detail in the following chapters. With a solid hermeneutical method in place the biblical counselor will work hard to understand the texts of Scripture rightly and to teach the proper interpretation to counselees.[12] With great hope and vision the compassionate counselor can give the counselee a sense of hope and trust in the timeless principles of God's Word that have guided and continue to guide the people of God throughout history, knowing that those who take to heart the full intent of the Scriptures devoid of their personal agendas will find the protection and answers they seek (Proverbs 30:5-6; 2 Timothy 3:16-17).

---

[12] The following are suggested as texts for the study of hermeneutics. *Knowing Scripture* by R. C. Sproul, InterVarsity Press, 1977; *He Gave Us Stories* by Richard Pratt, Wolgemuth and Hyatt Publishers, 1990; *The Inspiration and Authority of the Bible* by B. B. Warfield, Presbyterian and Reformed Publishing, 1970.

All Scripture is given by inspiration of God, and is profitable for doctrine, for reproof, for correction, for instruction in righteousness, that the man of God may be complete, thoroughly equipped for every good work (2 Timothy 3:16-17).

The sufficiency of the Bible as the voice of God

Even among Christians there is much debate as to the place of Scripture in counseling. Some believe that information extraneous to Scripture is necessary to successfully live the Christian life. It follows that without the benefit of modern psychiatry and psychology the Apostles and Christians of earlier ages were not all they could be in Christ.

Dr. Ed Bulkley makes a plea he addresses concerning the sufficiency of Scripture:

> As earnestly as I know how, I plead with you to understand this vital truth: God has provided answers in His Scriptures for every possible spiritual/mental/emotional problem that mankind *has ever* and *could ever* experience. There are no truly unique problems that modern man experiences. Sexual, verbal, and physical abuse have been with us since the days of Cain. Marriage problems, poor self-esteem, addictions of every sort, Attention Deficit Disorder, jealousy, violent rage, depression, and virtually every other psychological problem is recorded in biblical case histories.[13]

The Word of God *is* sufficient as the third answer of the Larger Catechism of the Westminster Confession of Faith states: *The holy Scriptures of the Old and New Testaments are the word of God, the only rule of faith and obedience.*[14]

---

[13] *Why Christians Can't Trust Psychology* by Ed Bulkley, Harvest House Publishing 1993, p. 277.
[14] See also the larger statement in the main body of the *Westminster Confession of Faith*, WCF I/vi.

Sufficiency defined

> The sufficiency of Scripture means that Scripture contained
> all the words of God he intended his people to have at
> each stage of redemptive history, and that it now contains
> all the words of God we need for salvation, for trusting
> him perfectly, and for obeying him perfectly.[15]

Sufficient for what?

God has called Christians to live up to the high calling they
have received (Ephesians 4:1) and He has not left His people
without the necessary provision of His Word to do so. It is in
accord with His character as Creator, Father, Savior and Guide
that He would not leave us without instruction. The Apostle
Peter summarizes this concept:

> Grace and peace be multiplied to you in the knowledge of
> God and of Jesus our Lord, as His divine power has given to
> us all things that pertain to life and godliness, through the
> knowledge of Him who called us by glory and virtue, by
> which have been given to us exceedingly great and precious
> promises, that through these you may be partakers of the
> divine nature, having escaped the corruption that is in the
> world through lust (2 Peter 1:2-4).

The Apostle Paul declared that the Word of God makes one
wise unto salvation as it is applied by faith in the person of God:
*and that from childhood you have known the Holy Scriptures, which
are able to make you wise for salvation through faith which is in
Christ Jesus. All Scripture is given by inspiration of God, and is
profitable for doctrine, for reproof, for correction, for instruction in
righteousness, that the man of God may be complete, thoroughly
equipped for every good work* (2 Timothy 3:15-17).

---

[15] *Systematic Theology* by Wayne Grudem, Zondervan Publishing, 1994, p. 128.

Sufficient to train in all things pertaining to life and godliness means that we find within Scripture all the commands and principles necessary for people to live honorable lives with increasing conformity to God's ideal. *And we, who with unveiled faces all reflect the Lord's glory, are being transformed into his likeness with ever increasing glory, which comes from the Lord, who is the Spirit* (2 Corinthians 3:18 NIV).

As Pastor Bob Hoekstra writes: *God wants us declaring, living, believing, growing in and passing on to one another this great foundation stone of the faith, the sufficiency of the Word of God. It is sufficient to make of our lives what God wants our lives to be: saved, sanctified, liberated, complete, fully equipped for service.*[16]

Do not add to His words!

The Bible is sufficient and as His sufficient word man must be careful to add nothing to or take anything away from the teaching of Scripture. In their book, *A Holy Rebellion*, Thomas Ice and Robert Dean, Jr. make the following comment:

Rather than taking the Bible alone, many people today are merging the divine viewpoint of the Bible with the human viewpoint of psychology or sociology or self-help techniques. They are trying to solve the problems in their lives not by Christ alone, but by Christ plus something else. This has left them dangerously handicapped in carrying out their rebellion against Satan. In fact, by taking the Bible plus something else they are doing what Satan wants them to do.[17]

To add to His Word is to say that what we have in the revelation of God is not adequate to train people in salvation and discipleship. No science or social study can delve into the heart of man with certainty as the Word of God can do. To take the findings of any discipline of academic endeavor and hold

---

[16] *The Psychologizing of the Faith* by Bob Hoekstra, The Word for Today Publishing, 1997, p. 45.

[17] *A Holy Rebellion* by Thomas Ice and Robert Dean, Jr., Harvest House Publishing, 1990, pp. 140-141.

those findings above the truth revealed in Scripture is to deny the truth and feed the lie of Satan. Remember that when Eve was confronted by the Serpent she added to the words of God. God had said:

> And the LORD God commanded the man, saying, "Of every tree of the garden you may freely eat; but of the tree of the knowledge of good and evil **you shall not eat**, for in the day that you eat of it you shall surely die" (Genesis 2:16-17, emphasis added).

> And the woman said to the serpent, "We may eat the fruit of the trees of the garden; but of the fruit of the tree which is in the midst of the garden, God has said, 'You shall not eat it, **nor shall you touch it**, lest you die.'" (Genesis 3:2-3 NKJV, emphasis added).

It will seem to some that the addition by Eve, *nor shall you touch it*, is a small addition. But we offer two possibilities for consideration: 1) Eve either did not know God's Word well enough or did not hold it, or Him, in high enough esteem, or 2) her addition is an indication that she wanted what the Serpent was offering and was seeking to show God to be unfair.

Commentators Keil and Delitzsch offer the following observation:

> She was aware of the prohibition, therefore, and fully understood its meaning; but she added, "neither shall ye touch it," and proved by this very exaggeration that it appeared too stringent even to her, and therefore that her love and confidence toward God were already beginning to waiver.[18]

The Serpent attacked God's words and tried to show Eve that He must not have meant what she thinks He said. Many of

---

[18] *Commentary on the Old Testament, Vol. 1,* by Keil and Delitzsch, Eerdman's Publishing, 1983, p. 95.

the counselees we face are looking for justification from an "authority" such as the counselor to do what they have already determined they want to do. The truly compassionate counselor will not allow this to happen. It would, in effect, give them an excuse to sin. To give someone an excuse for sin based on some observation of psychology or sociology or simply because we feel sorry for them is not to show compassion. The healing God offers is from the effects of sin. To treat the disease as anything else is to lie to the person and to add to God's words. Notice God's stern warnings from the following examples:

• "You shall not add to the word which I command you, nor take from it, that you may keep the commandments of the LORD your God which I command you" (Deuteronomy 4:2).
• "Whatever I command you, be careful to observe it; you shall not add to it nor take away from it" (Deuteronomy 12:32).
• "Every word of God is pure; He is a shield to those who put their trust in Him. Do not add to His words, lest He rebuke you, and you be found a liar" (Proverbs 30:5-6).
• "... as also our beloved brother Paul, according to the wisdom given to him, has written to you, as also in all his epistles, speaking in them of these things, in which are some things hard to understand, which untaught and unstable people twist to their own destruction, as they do also the rest of the Scriptures" (2 Peter 3:15-16).
• "For I testify to everyone who hears the words of the prophecy of this book: If anyone adds to these things, God will add to him the plagues that are written in this book; and if anyone takes away from the words of the book of this prophecy, God shall take away his part from the Book of Life, from the holy city, and from the things which are written in this book" (Revelation 22:18-19).

In the areas in which God's Word speaks we must be very careful to speak the truth. We do harm to those we seek to help if we speak anything other than the truth.

CHAPTER 3

THE BIBLE AS LIVING AND DYNAMIC

The Word of God is not simply a cognitive exercise. We are not advocating reciting Scripture as though it were a secret mantra. It is much more than literature. The Word of God, the Bible, is said to be alive and powerful. It is God's Word, at work in the believer through the ministry of the Holy Spirit that brings about a fundamental change in the person. How does the Word take root within the heart of a person and help him grow in Christ? We can discover the answers in the letter to the Hebrews.

A quick review of chapters 3 and 4 of Hebrews will help set the stage. Here we discovered that the Israelites did not enter God's rest because they missed out on a few key elements needed to enter God's rest. They did not combine faith and obedience. It is reflected clearly when the writer says in 3:18-19, *And to whom did He swear that they would not enter His rest, but to those who **did not obey**? So we see that they could not enter in **because of unbelief*** (emphasis added). It is interesting to note that obedience and unbelief are interchanged. They did not enter because they did not obey; they could not enter because of unbelief. Obedience and unbelief are interchanged. This is a particularly interesting connection as we consider the life-giving properties of God's Word. We want those we try to help to believe from the heart so that they will be truly changed (Ephesians 6:6; 1 Timothy 1:5). We do not want them to be included in the warning of verse 11, *Let us therefore be diligent to enter that rest, lest anyone fall according to the same example of disobedience.*

With the warning of verse 11 in mind the writer goes directly to a discussion of the Word of God and its life-giving properties.

The principle is clear that if we want to assure ourselves of not falling short in disobedience we need a relationship with the Word of God such as is described in the following verses. With that in mind we will examine these words.

The Word of God is living ...
God's Word has life-giving properties. When combined with faithful obedience (see also verses 3:18-19; 4:6-7) it has the effect of growing within us, producing spiritual life for those who partake of it in faith. As God's living Word has its effect in me, it will drive out evil practices and attitudes and replace them with something that is living and vital and comes from the very heart of God. In 1 Peter 1:23, Peter says that, ... *having been born again, not of corruptible seed but incorruptible, through the Word of God which lives and abides forever....* Peter too, refers to God's Word as living.

The Word of God is powerful ...
God's Word is living and it is also powerful, or active. The word from which *powerful* comes is the same root word from which we get the word *energy*. There is an energy to God's Word so that it accomplishes what it is supposed to do. As Isaiah spoke of God's words he said: *So shall My word be that goes forth from My mouth; It shall not return to Me void, But it shall accomplish what I please, And it shall prosper in the thing for which I sent it* (55:11).

Just as God spoke the creation into being with the power of His Word: *By the Word of the* LORD *the heavens were made, And all the host of them by the breath of His mouth.... For He spoke, and it was done; He commanded, and it stood fast* (Psalm 33:6, 9). God creates with the power of His Word. If His Word can create the world, the cosmos, and everything in it, His Word can certainly do in us what it is meant to do.

The Word of God is sharper than any two-edged sword ...
The Word is said to be a sword in Ephesians 6:17 as part of the armor used in spiritual warfare. The use of the sword metaphor

is apt since it is a weapon that can be both offensive and defensive. As the sword was used to block the blows of the opponent's sword it was also used to thrust a blow into the body. So it is with the Word of God. Jesus used the Word when resisting the devil in the wilderness (Matthew 4). When Peter faithfully proclaimed the Word of God in the sermon on Pentecost the response of those who heard was telling: *Now when they heard this, they were cut to the heart, and said to Peter and the rest of the apostles, "Men and brethren, what shall we do?"* (Acts 2:37).

God's Word *is* sharp. It can destroy or do the delicate surgery that the spiritual heart needs. Which brings us to the next image used....

The Word of God ... piercing even to the division of soul and spirit ...

This sword pierces in such a way so as to divide in the most minute detail. The point of the image is to say that that which man cannot distinguish the Word of God can. God knows what needs to be done and His Word can accomplish the task.

The Word of God ... is a discerner of the thoughts and intents of the heart ...

Not only does the Word dig deep, not only does it cut both ways but it is capable of uncovering and bringing forth our true motives. *And there is no creature hidden from His sight, but all things are naked and open to the eyes of Him to whom we must give account* (Hebrews 4:13). This uncovering is important for what disease can be cured if it is not first of all correctly diagnosed. Perhaps the reader has seen this lived out as a person comes to grips with the depth of his own sinfulness before a holy God. We have seen an awareness of personal sin bring a flood of tears that touches the heart of the most calloused person. But it is also our experience that when the reality of the depth of God's merciful grace is understood to completely cover that sin, the relief and joy is indescribable. God calls us to account. It is compassionate to expose sin because we can lead them to a most merciful God who will deal with their sin in a most gracious way if they are open to His mercy.

But how do we lead them to this understanding? The skilled counselor will use the Word of God to do so. For all our persuasive speech we are no match for the living Word. Show them their sin in the Word of God and, as they begin to see, show them the provision of a merciful heavenly Father who has provided a way out of their condemnation (Romans 5:8; 8:1).

The result of God's Word at work is freedom ...
The Psalmist declares the freedom that is found in God's Word:

- I will walk about in freedom, for I have sought out your precepts (119:45 NIV).

- Your word is a lamp to my feet and a light for my path (119:105 NIV).

- Great peace have they who love your law, and nothing can make them stumble (119:165 NIV).

This freedom is the freedom to love and enjoy God by faith (Hebrews 11:1, 6) by the person who has been freed from the reign of sin in his life (Romans 6).

The result of God's Word at work is knowledge of God's will...
We know God by combining information about God with faithful obedience (Romans 12:1-2; Hebrews 11:6). The Apostle tells us: *I beseech you therefore, brethren, by the mercies of God, that you present your bodies a living sacrifice, holy, acceptable to God, which is your reasonable service. And do not be conformed to this world, but be transformed by the renewing of your mind, that you may prove what is that good and acceptable and perfect will of God* (Romans 12:1-2). As a man's mind is renewed by the Word of God combined with holy living, he will be changed and begin to think more and more

like Christ and live in a way which is consistent with His will. In the discourse of Jesus concerning the truth He made it clear that knowledge of the truth requires the obedience of a true disciple. *Then Jesus said to those Jews who believed Him, "If you abide in My Word, you are My disciples indeed. And you shall know the truth, and the truth shall make you free"* (John 8:31-32).

It is our experience that counselees often want to know the answer to their problems without knowing God. The counselor must not give in to the desire, no matter how well intentioned, of letting the counselee seek happiness or contentment above obedience and true discipleship. True freedom – the freedom to love and enjoy God in the performance of His will – is experienced through the true knowledge of God and His Word. It requires hard work and faithful commitment.

The result of God's Word at work is devotion to the living God

Those who are made alive by the work of the Word of God in their lives are not to flaunt their freedom or use it in some way unbecoming the Lord (Ephesians 4:1) but they are to live in gratitude to the God who has set them free. As we read in the following portions of Scripture:

• Then those who gladly received His Word were baptized; and that day about three thousand souls were added to them. And they continued steadfastly in the apostles' doctrine and fellowship, in the breaking of bread, and in prayers (Acts 2:41-42).

• O wretched man that I am! Who will deliver me from this body of death? I thank God; through Jesus Christ our Lord! (Romans 7:24-25).

• Act as free men, and do not use your freedom as a covering for evil, but use it as bondslaves of God (1 Peter 2:16).

Who can flee from the Spirit?[19]

The writer in Hebrews 4:13 goes on to say that, *there is no creature hidden from his sight, but all things are naked and open to the eyes of him to whom we must give account* (NIV). We try to hide. Perhaps it is because we seek to keep our own agendas as opposed to God's agenda, but to what avail? Is it that God doesn't know? Certainly not, but counselees will often hide behind their reasons often thinking that these "reasons" are legitimate excuses for their sin. It may not be that they are truly thinking God doesn't know about them but they may simply not care, or their walk with God is at such an immature state that His knowledge of them is simply not real to them. For most, they know God knows but they get busy or so self-involved that they do not have to think about it.

The verse here is making it clear that no one can hide. It is the responsibility of the counselor to sensitively make the issues clear to the counselee. Timing is important but we must not let them believe the lie that they can hide or that God does not see or that He does not care.

James 1:22 tells us to be hearers of the Word but to also be doers of the Word. Hearing and doing is a connection made by faith. We must be about doing what the Word says while trusting God to accomplish His purposes whether or not we see immediate results.

God's surgery is almost always painful but it is necessary and the result is health, healing, growing up to be the child of God that He desires us to be and bringing great pleasure to His heart. There are no other options if we desire to obey Him. God is God and if we are truly His children, we want to grow up to be like our Heavenly Father. His Word, active in our hearts, is the way to accomplish that. There is no other way to discover the truth. There is no other way to experience His peace. There is no other way to please Him. The effective and compassionate counselor will focus on God's Word as that which can, combined with faith, change a person.

---

[19] See Psalm 139 on running from God.

CHAPTER 4

THE BIBLE AS A COUNSELING TOOL

If someone goes to work as a mechanic he is often required to own his own tools. It is not enough, however, to have just any tools; he must have the right tools for the job. Trying to do a job without the right tool often leads to frustration if not complete failure. The biblical counselor needs his tools to be adequate as a counselor. The primary tool is the Word of God. In this chapter we will look at various aspects of the Word in order to gain a perspective as to the vast array of "tools" at our disposal in the Bible.

Some have criticized those in biblical counseling by complaining that we simplistically use favorite Bible verses with those who are hurting without regard for the depth of their problems. Perhaps some do but what we are advocating is anything but simplistic. The biblical counselor does not indiscriminately use Scripture as though it were a mystical mantra nor do we use it as a hammer to pound truth into people. The biblical counselor should be a mature person (see chapters 6–8) who sees the battle in the counseling office as a battle against all that a person is, including his history, his intellect, his will, his depth of understanding of scripture and certainly his standing before God in terms of salvation. We also understand that the battle is very much a battle in the spiritual realm (Ephesians 6:12) and that we are utterly dependent upon the work of the Holy Spirit in the person's life to apply the Word of God effectively.[20] With that in mind, we want to take an overview of

---

[20] See John 16 as Jesus explains the need for the Holy Spirit.

the Bible as a counseling tool in that we want to get a sense of the types of issues to which it speaks.[21]

The Word of God is for discipleship

When Paul wrote to young Timothy he wanted to impress upon him the importance of the Word in discipleship. All Scripture is given by the inspiration of God, and is profitable for doctrine, for reproof, for correction, for instruction in righteousness, that the man of God may be complete, thoroughly equipped for every good work (2 Timothy 3:16-17). Let's take a brief look at the parts of these verses.

First we see that all Scripture is inspired or more literally "God breathed". It is the very breath of God giving life spiritually just as He gave Adam life physically when He breathed into Adam's nostrils the breath of life. Coming from Him in such an intimate way the word should revive and refresh the soul as fresh clean air refreshes the body. Timothy is taught several uses of the Word which deserve our special attention.[22]

The Word of God is profitable for doctrine/teaching ... what we need to learn concerning discipleship we can learn from scripture. Peter echoed a similar teaching in 2 Peter 1:3 when he tells us that knowledge of God gives us everything we need for life and godliness. We know God through His self-revelation.

The Word of God is profitable for reproof/rebuke ... sinful man needs to be warned of the dangers of sin. Errors in doctrine and conduct must be addressed.

The Word of God is profitable for correction ... It is not enough to point out error. We must show the right thing to do. This is very positive as it does not leave the sinner in judgment but

---

[21] There are various resources for finding what portions of Scripture speak to various problems. We recommend the following as a starting point: *A Quick Scripture Reference for Counseling, Second Edition* by John Kruis, Baker Book House; *Christian Counselor's New Testament* by Jay Adams, Timeless Texts; *Topical Guide to the Bible*, Walter Elwell ed., Baker Book House.
[22] See *New Testament Commentary: Thessalonians, Timothy and Titus* by William Hendriksen, Baker Book House, 1983.

takes him to a new place of righteousness. It is much the same principle of Ephesians 4 where Paul tells them to put-off the old man (reproof) and put-on the new man (correction) through the renewing of the mind (see also Romans 12:1-2).

The Word of God is profitable for instruction in righteousness ... That is what the disciple is to do – become increasingly righteous. In order to accomplish this the teacher or discipler needs to bring all scripture to bear on the disciple for reproof of those things about which he needs to be warned and for correction, so that he might get it right to the end that he would be equipped to do all God would have him do.

The Word of God then is indispensable in this process. We do not need secular theories or the latest technique to get us what we want in life. We need God's Word working in our hearts to make us more like Christ.

More precious than gold

Psalm 19 is a song written by King David and is another portion of Scripture that serves as a wonderful discourse on the beauty, durability, and usefulness of the Word to help people become the kind of people who are pleasing to God and are thus able to enjoy Him in abundance. We have already seen the dual speech contained in this Psalm as verses 1-6 speak of what the heavens declare about the Creator (see chapter 1). Here we will focus on the part of the Psalm that deals with His special revelation, His written Word, and its application to the counseling process.[23]

The law of the LORD is perfect, converting the soul ...

The law or teaching of God's Word is fully complete, lacking nothing and able to do all it was intended to do. Contained within the Word is all man needs for conversion and for the revival of his soul.

---

[23] The following commentaries on Psalm 19 have been helpful in this study: *Spurgeon's Treasury of David, Vol. I,* Baker Book House, 1984; *Commentary on the Old Testament, Psalms* by Keil and Delitzsch, Eerdman's, 1986; *Psalms of Promise* by Calvin Beisner, NavPress, 1988; *Our Sufficiency in Christ* by John F. MacArthur, Crossway Books, 1991.

The testimony of the LORD is sure, making wise the simple...
Scripture is the divine witness of God and is reliable. We can trust its precepts as timeless. It is reliable to make even the most simple wise unto salvation. Paul spoke in such terms to Timothy concerning the power and sufficiency of God's Word, ... *and that from childhood you have known the Holy Scriptures, which are able to make you wise for salvation through faith which is in Christ Jesus* (2 Timothy 3:15).

The statutes of the LORD are right, rejoicing the heart ...
The Scriptures contain specific precepts that are true and faithful. Adherence to them brings rejoicing to the heart. As we find specific commands in Scripture, taking them seriously by faith will encourage and invigorate a person. For instance Paul says a person should not steal but rather he should work and share with others (Ephesians 4:28). When people work in a useful way they fulfill a mandate from God and experience a fulfillment that stealing could never bring. When their work is useful in the lives of others they experience an even greater delight in helping people. Here, simply put, God's specific command against stealing is coupled with what might be considered positive commands to bring to a person delight in the place of possible depression, worry, guilt, or a host of other emotions a thief might experience, not to mention the discipline of God.

The commandment of the LORD is pure, enlightening the eyes...
When we are told precisely what to do by one in authority there is no mystery nor are there any excuses. We know what to do. The way is clear. It is as though we were following detailed directions that are unpolluted with incorrect information and therefore pure. The result is that the way is clear and we reach our destination. Directions of this nature are meant to be followed precisely, and so followed will deliver us to the proper destination without mishap. Counselors will help their counselees see clearly as they unveil for them God's clear commands concerning the issues they face.

The fear of the LORD is clean, enduring forever ...

We are all called to fear or reverence God in a way that holds Him in highest esteem in our hearts and minds. There is also a very real sense in which we should be motivated to obedience based on the fear of disobedience. The Scriptures are full of warnings. The person who commits fornication could contract a fatal disease not only destroying his life but his testimony as a child of God as well. Living in reverential fear of God and His commands is clean in the sense that it is a way of life that keeps one pure and undefiled. As God's Word will always be true His people can trust that in every age it will be true. As Jesus said, *"Heaven and earth will pass away, but My words will by no means pass away"* (Mark 13:31). Theories of psychology will come and go but God's Word is true for all of time and eternity.

The judgments of the LORD are true and righteous altogether...

The divine verdicts of God are true. The Word of God is the standard for judgment of every life that has existed or will exist. The way to heaven has never changed and God's judgments are righteous. He is completely just in His verdicts and eventually every person will bow to the Savior (Philippians 2:9-11) in acknowledgment of His eternal Lordship. People must know that God does not look the other way, that every person will be judged in accord with the Word of God. Either we will be judged based on our own righteousness or the righteousness of Christ (Philippians 3:9). But beyond our own eternal destiny it is important that we stress the proper respect for the law of God which sees its usefulness in guiding us in righteous living so that we bring honor to God (Matthew 5:17-19; Romans 3:20, 31; 7; 8:1-4; Galatians 3:24).

More to be desired are they than gold ... Sweeter also than honey...

Many approach God's Word as a set of rules that spoil their fun. But God's children love Him and desire, in increasing measure, to please Him. But beyond love and obedience true children feast on His Word. They have an insatiable thirst that is quenched only through drinking deeply His words. As a young soldier at war longs for a letter from his bride back home and reads it over and over when it comes, so the child of God longs for the rich bounty and sweet desserts of His Word. For they are life to him.

It must be stressed that this is in ever increasing measure (2 Corinthians 3:18). The young Christian, while wide eyed and curious, has not developed the love and respect for the Word that will increase with age. The counselor must be respectful of the "age" of the counselee while pressing them onward toward Christ-likeness.

Moreover by them your servant is warned, and in keeping them there is great reward ...

Lest anyone become prematurely satisfied that they have arrived at a place in the Christian life of stagnation, which often masquerades as satisfaction, we have the warnings of Scripture as well as the promises. To be warned is to be loved by God. We do not warn one of danger if we desire them to be hurt. We warn because we care. God warns us of His timeless commands which must be kept. And which, if they are not kept, will do us harm. But He does more than that. He rewards us in many ways if we keep them, not the least of which is eternal salvation and joy in this present life which comes from knowing Him.

Our counselees may resent God's commands, seeking above all temporal happiness. We must admonish them to look seriously at God Himself as revealed in His Word to discover how joy can flow from a deep knowledge of and love for the Creator who has a plan for those who love Him in this life and beyond.

The claims of Scripture

The following are various claims from Scripture about Scripture which will serve as an overview to illustrate how indispensable Scripture is to the counseling process.

The Word of God is illuminating – Psalm 119:105; 130; 133; 2 Peter 1:19; 1 John 2:8.

The Word of God is inspired – Nehemiah 9:13; Acts 1:15; Romans 1:2; 1 Corinthians 4:35; Galatians 1:11; 1 Thessalonians 2:13; 2 Timothy 3:16; 1 Peter 1:10-12; 2 Peter 1:2-21.

The Word of God is instructive – Psalm 119:24, 169; Romans 15:4.

The Word of God is powerful – Jeremiah 23:29; Ephesians 6:17; 2 Timothy 2:8; Hebrews 4:12.

The Word of God is revelation – Exodus 24:4; Jeremiah 30:2; 45:1-2; Habakkuk 2:2; John 20:30; Revelation 22:18.

The Word of God is reliable – 1 Kings 8:56; Psalm 19:9; 105:19; Proverbs 22:19; Luke 24:44.

The Word of God is a safeguard – Psalm 17:4; 119:9, 11; Proverbs 3:5-6.

The Word of God is truth – Matthew 15:1-3; Mark 7:7-13; John 5:46-47; Acts 18:28; 28:23.

The Word of God is true – Psalm 33:4; 119:43, 151; Proverbs 22:20; John 17:7; Colossians 1:3-6; 2 Timothy 3:15; Revelation 19:9, 21:5.

The Word of God is trustworthy – Psalm 19:7; 111:7; 119:138; Revelation 22:6.

The Word applied

Application of God's Word is developed as the counselor grows in his or her personal knowledge of the Word and explores the various ways it is applied. The following is a homework assignment for those struggling with depression.[24] It is only one assignment with a series of questions to spur the counselee's thinking about his condition and to provide the counselor with information about how the counselee thinks about depression and how they process biblical truth as it applies to personal problems.

---

[24] Taken from *Homework CD for Biblical Counseling, Vol. 1* by Howard Eyrich and Bill Hines. Used by permission.

Questions Depressed People Should Ask
A Study Guide

1. Am I born again?
2. Do I hate sin?
3. Is my greatest desire to please God?
4. Do I believe that Jesus is the only Savior and that He is the only thing in which I trust for salvation?
5. Do I consistently practice righteousness?
6. Am I growing so that I am a different person today than I was last week or when I first believed in Christ?
7. Do I love other Christians and desire God's best for them even at personal cost?
8. Do I fear offending God more than I fear offending other people?
9. Do I strive for moral purity in daily living?
10. Am I willing to give up my depression in order to see life through His eyes?
11. Am I seeking to apply my mind to understanding God's Word as it relates to what I am experiencing?
12. Do I believe God's Word even when it conflicts with my experience?
13. Do I spend a great deal of time thinking about my past?
14. Do I exercise self-control?
15. Can I honestly say that He is my peace and deepest joy?
16. Have I learned to seek Him even when other matters seem more pressing?
17. Do I understand my complete acceptance of God is based on His grace?
18. Do I see my trials as an opportunity to show and learn faith?
19. When I am depressed am I willing to focus on Him rather than focusing on my problem?
20. Am I willing to act upon God's truth regardless of how I feel?
21. Am I committed to God's truth even if I "feel" it is not true?

THE BIBLE AS A COUNSELING TOOL

22. Do I continue to obey God even if I am feeling depressed?
23. Am I engaged in regular worship with other Christians?
24. Do I gather regularly with other Christians for fellowship?
25. Do I regularly take in the teaching and preaching of God's Word?
26. How often am I involved in ministering to other people?
27. How much time do I spend listening to "Christian" radio or watching "Christian" television a day?

Depression
A Study Guide

The following will act as a guide to look at what the Bible says about depression. Remember that while it is desirable to overcome depression this is best accomplished through understanding the depression and making a proper response to it. It should also be noted that the following assumes no physiological cause. A person experiencing severe depression should consult a physician to see if there is an organic cause or stimulus to the depression. But even if there is an organic connection the person must bear in mind that living in a state of depression often leaves behind inappropriate habits of thought and behavior which must be addressed.

a. Read the pamphlet *How to Handle Depression* by Jay Adams. This pamphlet stresses the thinking and behavior that often leads to depression. Be ready to discuss this with your counselor.

b. Keep a personal journal noting the times you experience depression. Be sure to note: the day and time it occurs; what triggers it; people involved; your response; what you ate that day (especially sweets) and anything else you consider important.

c. Using Psalm 139:23-24 as your guide, ask God to bring to mind any "hurtful ways" in you and write them down.

d. Study the following verses and list the things that could be circumstantial causes for depression.
   1. Psalm 32:3-4
   2. Psalm 73:1-14
   3. Genesis 4:6-7
   4. Deuteronomy 1:28-29
   5. Psalm 55:2-8
   6. 2 Samuel 18:33
   7. 1 Samuel 1:7-8
   8. Luke 24:17-21

e. According to Scripture we must both think right and act right in order to avoid depression (Philippians 4:8-9). From the following verses note what God says you must do to overcome your depression.

   1. Psalm 16:8-9
   2. Psalm 1:1-3
   3. Psalm 32:1-2
   4. John 13:17
   5. James 1:22-25
   6. Galatians 5:22-24
   7. Romans 15:13
   8. Acts 13:52
   9. Proverbs 15:23
   10. 1 Thessalonians 2:19-20

f. Make a list of the things you least enjoy doing. Make a list of the things you most enjoy doing.

g. What do you think would need to change for you to overcome depression? Be specific and include people, events, situations, etc.

CHAPTER 5

AN APPROACH THAT TARGETS THE HEART

What makes biblical counseling biblical? There are several things that could be pointed out. Much has already been said about this in previous chapters. But one area often overlooked concerns the focus or target of our counsel. For the sort of change to take place that is pleasing to God and has the power to truly change a person there must be a change of heart. In this chapter we will look at what it means to target the heart in counseling. We will do this through a discovery of what the heart is, why it is important, of what it is capable and how it is changed.

What is the heart of man?

In order to express the innermost core of man's being the Bible uses the word "heart". Dick Keyes offers the following practical definition for heart: *The inmost core of the self, your psychological and spiritual center of gravity.*[25] Theologian John Frame offers an explanation worth quoting at length:[26]

> The knowledge of God is a heart-knowledge (see Exodus 35:5; 1 Samuel 2:1; 2 Samuel 7:3; Psalm 4:4; 7:10; 15:2; Isaiah 6:10; Matthew 5:8; 12:34; 22:37; Ephesians 1:18, etc.). The heart is the "center" of the personality, the person himself in his most basic character. Scripture represents it as the source of thought, of volition, of attitude, of speech. It is also the seat of moral knowledge. In the Old

---

[25] *Beyond Identity* by Dick Keyes, Servant Books, 1984, p. 145.
[26] *The Doctrine of the Knowledge of God* by John Frame, Presbyterian & Reformed Publishing, 1987, p. 322.

Testament, **heart** is used in contexts where **conscience** would be an acceptable translation (see 1 Samuel 24:5).

This definition is similar to that given in *The MacArthur Study Bible*'s note at Proverbs 4:21-23 which reads:

> The "heart" commonly refers to the mind as the center of thinking and reason (3:3; 6:21; 7:3), but also includes the emotions (15:15, 30), the will (11:20; 14:14), and thus, the whole inner being (3:5). The heart is the depository of all wisdom and the source of whatever affects speech (v. 24), sight (v. 25), and conduct (vv. 26, 27).

As these definitions illustrate, "heart" is a broad term including much more than the romantic sense of the seat of the emotions alone. It is important that we understand that man is more than his behavior or feelings. A comprehensive approach to counseling from a biblical point of view will include the behavioral and emotional aspects but will see those aspects of man as flowing from the heart. They are the result of, not the cause of, who man is. In preparation for our look at the inner workings of the heart it is important to review the heart without Christ and the promise of a new heart.

The heart without Christ
There is a dark truth about man. Because of this truth he can never with credibility claim, "I did not mean it," or, "I didn't know what I was saying,' for the truth is we, in some sense, mean what we say. It may be that through years of habituation to a particular pattern of life that sin has become "natural" and we do things "without thinking". But we cannot use the excuses outlined above because that which we express in word or deed is what is within us. Jesus said as much:

> And He said, "What comes out of a man, that defiles a man. For from within, out of the heart of men, proceed evil thoughts, adulteries, fornications, murders, thefts,

covetousness, wickedness, deceit, lewdness, an evil eye, blasphemy, pride, foolishness. All these evil things come from within and defile a man (Mark 7:20-23).

The heart without Christ is a heart that is depraved. Frame puts it this way:[27]

> The fact that the heart is depraved, then, means that apart from grace we are in radical ignorance of the things of God. *There is no spiritual life or light in the heart without Christ* (1 Corinthians 1:18, 2:14).

We can look at key areas of life and see the expression of the sin nature:

• **Behavior** is an indicator of that which resides in the heart... *Do not turn to the right or the left; Remove your foot from evil* (Proverbs 4:27).

If I am willing to behave badly it is because it is within my heart to do so. No one makes me – I am tempted because within my heart I am temptable!

• **Feelings** are indicators of that which resides in the heart ... *All the days of the afflicted are evil, But he who is of a merry heart has a continual feast* (Proverbs 15:15). *The light of the eyes rejoices the heart, And a good report makes the bones healthy* (Proverbs 15:30).

If I am consumed with fear or unrighteous anger or anxiety it is because there is a lack of trust for God in my heart or I have not applied His Word to my situation.

• **Attitudes are indicators of that which resides in the heart** ... *Happy is the man who is always reverent, But he who hardens his heart will fall into calamity* (Proverbs 28:14). *Trust in the LORD with all your heart, And lean not on your own*

---

[27] Frame, p. 322.

understanding; In all your ways acknowledge Him, And He shall direct your paths (Proverbs 3:5-6, NKJV).

Basic attitudes such as trust, humility, reverence, fear and anger flow from the heart.

While any of these indicators may be in response to a variety of stimuli the response is that which flows from a heart based on its predisposition.

The promise of a new heart

For man to change he needs a new paradigm for life. It is not enough to simply behave differently or feel differently. If it were, there are various medications that could accomplish that. What man needs is a fundamental change that changes his motivations. Man needs a new heart.

We find in the prophets the promise of the new heart that would be accomplished by Messiah. This is such an incredible promise, such a great prophecy that God Himself is going to clean up our hearts and make them acceptable to Him. Here is a classic passage on the promise:

> "Then I will sprinkle clean water on you, and you shall be clean; I will cleanse you from all your filthiness and from all your idols. I will give you a new heart and put a new spirit within you; I will take the heart of stone out of your flesh and give you a heart of flesh. I will put My Spirit within you and cause you to walk in My statutes, and you will keep My judgments and do them. Then you shall dwell in the land that I gave to your fathers; you shall be My people, and I will be your God" (Ezekiel 36:25-28, NKJV).

This is such an amazing promise exhibiting the richness of His grace because we see that the work of giving a new heart is the work and gift of God Himself.

Volumes have been written on the subject of how the work of Christ is applied to man. For our purposes here we will offer a quick summary to spur your thinking about helping counselees realize the new heart which was promised through Ezekiel.[28]

The work of Christ involves not only His death on the cross and His resurrection, but it involves His sinless life, qualifying Him as a lamb without blemish, His perfect obedience to the Father to the point of death, His triumph over death at the resurrection, His ascension to the right hand of the Father, and His glorification making the way clear for the whole person to be received in heaven.

The work of Christ, then, is because man is in need. Our counselees feel guilty primarily because they *are* guilty before a holy God. Modern therapies would try to remove the guilt but the compassionate biblical counselor will explain that there is a good reason for the guilt feelings and there is great hope of redemption through the forgiveness of sins. Guilt, however, while it is a powerful emotion is not the only reason one should seek redemption. Christianity is truth and God deserves our worship simply because He is God and we are not. In a consumer-oriented society people often think of God and the Church as a commodity. To some, God is supposed to "be there" for them rather than seeing themselves in the position of "being there" to serve God. Yet it should be noted that God not only demands our worship based on His being God but He establishes a loving relationship and gives us a heart that is capable of loving Him. It could be likened to two fathers; one who says, *Obey me because I am your father*, and the other who takes the time to build a loving relationship that draws the child to love him.

---

[28] The following are popular works which we have found helpful in understanding the work of Christ as it is applied to the heart: *Redemption Accomplished and Applied* by John Murray, Banner of Truth Trust; *The Cross of Christ* by John Stott, InterVarsity Press; *True Spirituality* by Francis A. Schaeffer; *The Finished Work of Christ* by Francis A. Schaeffer, Crossway Books; *The Cross – The Vindication of God* (booklet) by D. Martyn Lloyd-Jones, Banner of Truth Trust. See also the list of works on *Systematic Theology* in chapter 6.

The condition of the new heart

Before a person is a Christian it is proper to think of him as one who is in need of evangelism since he does not have the ability to discern spiritual things (1 Corinthians 2:14-15). Taking him through passages such as 1 Corinthians 2:14-15, Romans 1:18-32 and 1 Corinthians 15 is an appropriate way to help him understand the basics of the gospel and his need to avoid the mistake of further suppressing the truth of God that is evident to all men.

Our call to care for the heart

Once you are certain you are dealing with a believer or one who believes he is a believer, you can move forward with counsel that seeks to change the heart. Several fundamental truths are spoken of in Proverbs 4:20-23 that are essential to growing into Christ-likeness. The condition of the new heart in a person still given to sin this side of heaven is such that he should be diligent in his pursuit of change. The counselor must help him understand that he must:

• **Be alert** (v. 20) ... Giving attention to the Word and wisdom of God, always listening, always understanding what is needed. Wisdom will tell us what is needed if we are seeking it, watching for it and applying it. Remember Jesus said that it was not just the one who knows what to do who is wise but he who knows what to do and does it (Matthew 7:24-29; James 1:22-25).

• **Incline the ear** (v. 20) ... Used here means to bow the ear or lean in to hear intently.

• **See what is needed** (v. 21) ... The words of God are to be kept in view at all times. As James explains we should not be among those who view the Word as a mirror, forgetting what we saw as soon as we turn away. We should continue to look intently at His law and put it into practice. *But he who looks into the perfect law of liberty and continues in it, and is not a forgetful hearer but a doer of the word, this one will be blessed in what he does* (James 1:25).

• **Fill the heart with the wisdom of God** (vv. 21, 23) ... Keep them in the midst of your heart; protect them in the center of your heart, the center of your being. The idea is that all that we are flows from the center of our being.

We should note that in all these things it has not been said that we should always be happy or without struggle. What is being said is that when God's Word resides in our hearts we live by faith and faith has its effect in all that we are.

• **Must be directed toward godly pursuits** (v. 23) ... To keep the heart with diligence is to be directed in godly pursuits. It is a responsibility to pursue holiness which keeps the heart pure or undivided. Paul, too, speaks of directing the heart: *Now may the Lord direct your hearts into the love of God and into the patience of Christ* (2 Thessalonians 3:5).

It is imperative to keep the heart in a diligent or disciplined way for it is the spring from which all matters flow. We cannot stress this enough in counseling. We must teach our counselees that they must work hard at directing their hearts in godly pursuits. To neglect the work of discipleship in one's heart is like failing to refuel before the last leg of a flight. It is foolish and leads to ruin. The counselor is, therefore, called upon to make certain that the counselee is not seeking to simply kill the pain when surgery is required. To help someone feel better while neglecting the real disease is wrong. The counselee may reject the counsel and even the counselor but we are to fear God not man (Luke 12:4-5). We are not to tell them what they want to hear at the expense of what they need to hear (2 Timothy 4:2-5). But in all these things we must keep clearly in view the instruction of Paul on how to confront the sinner: *Brethren, if a man is overtaken in any trespass, you who are spiritual restore such a one in a spirit of gentleness, considering yourself lest you also be tempted. Bear one another's burdens, and so fulfill the law of Christ* (Galatians 6:1-2).

Blessed are the pure in heart for they shall see God

To be pure in heart (Matthew 5:8) is to have a heart that is undivided in devotion to God. This takes work. This takes commitment. The counselor must have a pure heart and then he will be able to share his path to purity with his counselees. Is it ever perfect this side of heaven? No. However, it is increasingly being purified if we are people who love God. That is because the person who loves God never gives up (1 Corinthians 13) in his faithful pursuit of righteousness. We want our counselees to be such people which is why we must work that much harder to show them Christ in us and why we must not settle for anything less than change in the heart. To settle for less is not love.

Knowing the will of God is a matter of the heart

In his excellent work on knowing the will of God, Dr. Bruce Waltke makes a powerful observation concerning the heart:

> God wants you to be a mature man or woman of God – that is *His will for your Life!* He wants to see your character develop. He wants you to draw close to Him and be changed. We have the Holy Spirit in a *fuller* measure than the Old Testament saints, and He develops our character. This is why God terminated the Old Testament means of divination. Divining is a shortcut to the future, and God offers Christians no shortcuts. Divination sounds pious, but it may actually be ungodly because it shortcuts the Spirit's work in developing our character. It assumes you can know God's mind without having His heart and His Spirit. But discerning the mind of God cannot be done apart from character development. You cannot divine God's heart, but you have available to you a way to develop a heart like His. He can work in your life through the Holy Spirit and His Word to foster virtue, and then you will have the mind of Christ.[29]

---

[29] *Finding the Will of God*, by Bruce Waltke, 1995, Vision House Publishers.

SECTION TWO

THE NEED FOR A
BIBLICAL COUNSELOR

I was asked to consult with a psychiatrist whose patient I was counseling. He was a very nice man who I'm sure was a fine physician. When we began to talk he was very quick to say, "I'm a Jew, so I understand the spiritual side of things." But did he? We believe that only those who know God on a personal basis, having been born again by the Spirit through faith in the finished work of Christ, are spiritual. According to Scripture, all others are "natural" and do not understand the things of the Spirit (1 Corinthains 2:6-16). While it has become popular to talk about the spiritual aspects of man on television talk shows and twelve-step groups, only those who possess the Spirit of God can understand the things of the Spirit. And only those with a consistently biblical understanding can adequately counsel from a biblical perspective.

We would like to take this a step further, however, to make it clear that the biblical counselor is much more than one who knows biblical answers to life's questions. The biblical counselor is one who knows the Bible well and lives what he knows.

In this section we will explore the biblical counselor in terms of who he or she is as a theologian, as a person gifted for the work of counseling, and as one who possesses the character necessary to represent God to others.

CHAPTER 6

THE COUNSELOR AS
THEOLOGIAN

It has been our observation that much of what passes for biblical or Christian counseling flows from a study or an awareness of popular ideas with Bible verses tacked on. The biblical counselor is not one who simply learns "how" to counsel with Bible verses nor is he one who reduces a person's problems to theological slogans, pet doctrines or the most recent popular theories. The truly biblical counselor understands that he is a theologian. Does that mean he will attend seminary or Bible College? It might, but it will certainly mean that he will not settle for a Sunday school knowledge of the Bible. He will be conversant on essential doctrines such as regeneration, justification, sanctification, repentance and forgiveness. Theology – understanding God and His universe and His ways of working in man – will be a passion.[30]

Presented below are several key areas in which the biblical counselor must pursue a deep understanding. The items listed are in no way to be considered exhaustive but rather illustrative of the sort of issues that are central to this work.

The goal of life
When asked what is the greatest commandment Jesus responded in the following way:

---

[30] The counselor should have quick access to a major work on Systematic Theology. The following are suggested by the authors: *Systematic Theology* by Louis Berkhof, Eerdman's; *Systematic Theology* by Charles Hodge, Eerdman's; *Systematic Theology* by Wayne Grudem, Zondervan; *A New Systematic Theology of the Christian Faith* by Robert Reymond, Thomas Nelson Publishing.

Jesus answered him, "The first of all the commandments is: "Hear, O Israel, the Lord our God, the Lord is one. And you shall love the Lord your God with all your heart, with all your soul, with all your mind, and with all your strength." This is the first commandment. And the second, like it, is this: "You shall love your neighbor as yourself." There is no other commandment greater than these" (Mark 12:29-32).

Counseling requires that the counselor stay focused. The counselees are often troubled with the problem at hand. They often simply want to feel better. They are most likely focused on the problem and how they feel about it. The compassionate counselor will stay focused on the answer so that he or she may help the counselee please God by loving Him and loving others above all else. If we let them continue in self-centeredness we rob them of the joy and help that comes from loving God and others. Remember the goal must not be to simply feel better. Feeling better is a wonderful by-product of doing the right thing by faith in the living God who deserves our worship and obedience. But it must not be allowed to become the goal.

Suffering and the character and power of God
People suffer this side of heaven. The counselor has to have a deep understanding of how a good, loving, all-powerful God would allow His children to suffer. Simplistic answers or answers that have not been thought through are not good enough. The counselee will see them as trite, as well he should. It is at the point of suffering that many reject God altogether. It is also through suffering that we have seen many come to a profound understanding of who God is and His place in their lives. The compassionate counselor will dig deep into the scriptures to understand the depth of this issue in his own life and for those he seeks to help.[31]

---

[31] We suggest study on the attributes and character of God as well as an exploration into God's providence. We find that difficulties emerge in those who feel a need to explain rather than understand God.

The work of Christ

What did Christ accomplish through the incarnation? The way we answer that question will relate not only to the evangelization of the counselee but it will answer such questions as: *How can I know I am saved? How can I know God is not angry with me? On what basis can I begin to love my spouse when I feel so little love for him/her? How do I deal with guilt?*

When we write of the finished work of Christ we are writing of all that He did to accomplish the will of the Father on behalf of those who would believe. This includes His sinless life, His obedience unto death as the final sacrifice, His resurrection and post-resurrection activities, His ascension and glorification, His reign in the hearts of those who believe, and the blessed hope of His return for those who believe.

The sonship of believers

The Apostle John writes:

> Behold what manner of love the Father has bestowed on us, that we should be called children of God! Therefore the world does not know us, because it did not know Him. Beloved, now we are children of God; and it has not yet been revealed what we shall be, but we know that when He is revealed, we shall be like Him, for we shall see Him as He is. And everyone who has this hope in Him purifies himself, just as He is pure (1 John 3:1-3 NKJV).

There is something about our identification as children of God and the knowledge that we will one day see Him clearly as He is which helps to purify the believer. Understanding sonship brings a profound sense of belonging for the Christian as he or she recognizes a new Father in God the Father, and new brothers and sisters in other Christians. It connects us with the Father in a way that the Apostle Paul describes in the most intimate terms when he says:

For you did not receive the spirit of bondage again to fear, but you received the Spirit of adoption by whom we cry out, "Abba, Father". The Spirit Himself bears witness with our spirit that we are children of God, and if children, then heirs; heirs of God and joint heirs with Christ, if indeed we suffer with Him, that we may also be glorified together (Romans 8:15-17).

This is a profound truth and one that, rightly understood and embraced, brings a new level of identity, intimacy, hope and awe between the person and God the Father. Helping people understand their adoption into the family of God and the benefits of that relationship can truly help change how they think about life.[32]

The heart of man

The importance of this area has been stated in chapter 5. We include it here to underscore its importance. If we do not properly understand the heart of man as he is born into this world and as He is born again in Christ we will not be able to properly understand man's struggle with sin and righteousness and thus we will not be able to help people achieve increasing transformation into Christ-likeness.

The work of the Spirit

I often hear the theologically astute espouse the indispensability of the Holy Spirit in the Christian life. They may go on to say that no one will truly learn unless the Holy Spirit is the teacher quickening it in the heart of the student. But do we really live that way? Our experience is that teachers and counselors all too quickly slip back to the academic application of truths that lack the power of a genuine work of God.

---

[32] For more on this subject of adoption see: *Children of the Living God* by Sinclair Ferguson, Banner of Truth; *Leaving Yesterday Behind* by William L. Hines, Christian Focus Publications; *Child of a King* by Mark Johnston, Christian Focus Publications.

The biblical counselor must understand the work of the Holy Spirit and must be experiencing that work in his or her own life. If we do have a proper understanding and experience of the Spirit we will have something to offer that is truly dynamic and living and full of hope. Without the Holy Spirit applying the word of God to the hearts of people we have little more than any secular counselor who offers the latest version of pop-psychology.

It would be helpful to be reminded of the work of the Holy Spirit on man's behalf as it especially relates to counseling:

- The Spirit has emotion: Isaiah 63:10; Ephesians 4:30
- The Spirit exercises volition: 1 Corinthians 12:11
- The Spirit can be blasphemed: Matthew 12:31
- The Spirit can be grieved: Ephesians 4:30
- The Spirit can be insulted: Hebrews 10:29
- The Spirit can be lied to: Acts 5:3
- The Spirit can be obeyed: Acts 10:19, 21
- The Spirit can be quenched: 1 Thessalonians 5:19
- The Spirit can be resisted: Acts 6:9; Acts 7:51
- The Spirit can be tested: Acts 5:9
- The Spirit convicts the world of guilt: John 16:8-11
- The Spirit glorifies Christ: John 16:14
- The Spirit guides into truth: John 16:13
- The Spirit intercedes: Romans 8:26-27
- The Spirit regenerates: John 3:3-5
- The Spirit restrains evil: Genesis 6:3-5
- The Spirit sanctifies: Romans 15:16; 1 Corinthians 6:11
- The Spirit exercises power: Judges 14:6; 1 Samuel 10:10; Luke 4:14; Romans 15:13
- The Spirit encourages: Acts 9:31
- The Spirit gives gifts: 1 Corinthians 12:7-11
- The Spirit leads: Matthew 4:1; Romans 8:14
- The Spirit teaches: Luke 12:12; John 14:26; 1 Corinthians 2:13
- The Spirit gives life: John 6:63; Romans 8:2; 1 Peter 3:18

- The Spirit sanctifies: Romans 15:16; 1 Corinthians 6:11; 2 Thessalonians 2:13; 1 Peter 1:2
- The Spirit seals: 2 Corinthians 1:22; 2 Corinthians 5:5; Ephesians 1:13; Ephesians 4:30

While not exhaustive these characteristics of the work of the Spirit certainly show His essential work for and in those who believe. The biblical counselor will become aware first of the Spirit's work in his or her own life and will work at becoming competent to explain the application of the Spirit's work in the life of the counselee.

The Christian life as a process

We should ask those we seek to help the question, "Why were you made alive in Christ?" The answers we receive will be varied. Whatever people may say we must maintain that He lived, He died, He was resurrected and ascended to the Father that we might echo the deep desire of the Apostle Paul as he stated it in verses 10-11 of Philippians 3:

> I want to know Christ and the power of his resurrection and the fellowship of sharing in his sufferings, becoming like him in his death, and so, somehow, to attain to the resurrection from the dead.

Do our counselees desire His power? True power will also involve attaining in some measure to the fellowship of His suffering and death to sin. This is the desire of the mature Christian (v. 15). Mature Christians understand that all the comfort, power and security this world can offer is but a drop of water in a desert compared with the riches of Christ. But how easily people abandon the battle.

If we understand that the Christian life is a process (Philippians 2:12-13; 2 Corinthians 3:18) we will teach the tools for progress in the Christian life. These tools will include a proper understanding of such doctrines as confession, repentance, forgiveness, the walk of faith, and the application of the work of Christ to everyday living. The counselee must not be allowed to continue to bounce between emotional extremes but rather must be taught to live in a steady progress toward Christ-likeness.[33]

The theologian is always learning

The biblical counselor must be a theologian. There must be a passion to know, experience and obey God in ever increasing measure. Always learning, always pressing on to know and experience God. It is in our capacity as a theologian who is in the process of growing up in Christ that we will be able to offer the real answers the Bible gives to those who desire our help.

---

[33] A proper understanding of the sanctification process will have a dramatic effect on the counseling ministry. Denominations differ widely and care should be taken to be certain that the approach adopted is truly biblical. For an overview of five views on sanctification see *Christian Spirituality* by Donald Alexander ed., InterVarsity Press, 1988.

CHAPTER 7

THE GIFTS OF THE COUNSELOR

Perhaps you are reading a book on counseling because you think you want to be a counselor. Why do you think you should pursue this kind of work? Perhaps it has been a desire for a long time. Perhaps you experienced something in your own life that has given you a passion to help others going through similar crises. Perhaps you are fascinated with the way people grow and change or you know it will help you in a related vocation. Most often it is a combination of these and other circumstances. Whatever your motivation, it is important for you to discover whether God has called you to do the work of a counselor. One way to help you to discover such a calling is to take a close look at the gifts we would expect the gifted counselor to possess.

Who is to counsel?

We begin with the question, "Who is to counsel?" The answer may surprise some for it is our understanding from Scripture that all Christians are to counsel some of the time. This comes from passages such as:

- *Brethren, if a man is overtaken in any trespass, you who are spiritual restore such a one in a spirit of gentleness, considering yourself lest you also be tempted* (Galatians 6:1). Here those who are spiritual or those who have some maturity as Christians should help restore the sinner.[34] This is a work that would be expected of the biblical counselor.

---

[34] See 1 Corinthians 2:15; 3:1-3 for a discussion on spirituality. In these passages we find that a spiritual person is one who 1) possesses the Spirit and 2) has achieved some level of maturity.

• *But you are a chosen generation, a royal priesthood, a holy nation, His own special people, that you may proclaim the praises of Him who called you out of darkness into His marvelous light* ... (1 Peter 2:9). Here Christians are referred to as a royal priesthood. The priest is one who represents the people to God and God to the people. As believer priests we all have a responsibility to intercede on behalf of our brothers and sisters. This is one aspect of the work of counseling. It should also be noted that this is not an option for the Christian. We are each priests and therefore we are to do the work of a priest.

Toward a definition of counseling

What is a biblical definition for counseling? In our day it is often the idea of caring or giving advice or helping people feel better. Many modern therapists warn their counseling students against telling people what to do. They think that to be directive is to impose on people some external truth and that it is better for people to "find" the truth within themselves. That is not the biblical idea of helping. There is absolute truth and people need to know what it is and they come to us because they do not have the answers. We need to care enough to tell them the truth. This is at the heart of our biblical definition and we find it expressed by the Apostle Paul in his letter to the Colossians:

And we proclaim Him, admonishing every man and teaching every man with all wisdom, that we may present every man complete in Christ (Colossians 1:28 NASB).

The key word here is the word "admonish". "Admonish" is an interesting and meaningfull word. Some translate it "counseling" but it is more than what we usually mean by counseling. Of the Apostle Paul's use of this word William Hendriksen says: "For [Paul] to admonish meant to warn, to stimulate and to encourage. He would actually plead with people to be reconciled to God (2 Corinthains 5:20). He would at times even shed tears (cf. Acts 20:19, 31: 2 Corinthians 2:4; Philippians 4:18)."[35] To warn people is to save them from the further agony of their sin. Stimulating them is to "stir up" or "agitate" within them the desire to pursue Christ-likeness. To encourage is to give them hope in a God of grace to fulfill His promises to His children. To engage in a ministry which seeks to warn, to stimulate and to encourage people to Christ-likeness is to do the work of biblical counseling.[36]

The gifts of the Spirit

The gifts are given by the Holy Spirit (1 Corinthians 12: 4, 7, 11; Hebrews 2:4) for the purpose of:

a. Active Use in the Church
Therefore I remind you to stir up the gift of God which is in you through the laying on of my hands (2 Timothy 1:6; see also 1 Corinthians 14:26; 1 Timothy 4:14). Gifts are for use. All Christians should be seeking and using their gifts for the benefit of others.

b. Building up of the Body of Christ
And He Himself gave some to be apostles, some prophets, some evangelists, and some pastors and teachers, for the equipping of the saints for the work of ministry, for the edifying of the body of Christ (Ephesians 4:11-12; see also Romans 12:3-6; 1 Corinthians 12:12-27; Ephesians 4:16). The gifts benefit the Church.

c. Serving Others
As each one has received a gift, minister it to one another, as good stewards of the manifold grace of God (1 Peter 4:10).

---

[35] *New Testament Commentary: Philippians, Colossians, and Philemon* by William Hendriksen. Baker Book House, 1985.

[36] The word or its root translated "admonish" here is also used in the following passages: Acts 20:31; Romans 15:14; 1 Corinthians 4:14; Colossians 1:28; Colossians 3:16; 1 Thessalonians 5:12, 14; 2 Thessalonians 3:15.

d. For the Common Good
But the manifestation of the Spirit is given to each one for the profit of all (1 Corinthians 12:7).

e. Equipping the Saints
And He Himself gave some to be apostles, some prophets, some evangelists, and some pastors and teachers, for the equipping of the saints for the work of ministry, for the edifying of the body of Christ (Ephesians 4:11-12).

The Holy Spirit equips people for work in the Kingdom of God. These gifts are given at His discretion and the recipients are to faithfully develop and use their gifts as a sacred trust from God. Years ago a pastor commented that: "The wise Christian will discover his spiritual gift and build his life around it." That is not to say that we all will be paid to use our gifts but it is to say that our jobs will support our use of those gifts.

The gifts of the counselor
While all are called to do the work of the counselor some of the time, some have a special calling and giftedness to do the work on a wider scale as a special calling. These are people who will be specially gifted by the Holy Spirit to do the work of counseling. Various lists of gifts are included in Romans 12:6-8, 1 Corinthians 12:4-11; Ephesians 4:11-13; 1 Peter 4:10-11.

As each one has received a gift, minister it to one another, as good stewards of the manifold grace of God. If anyone speaks, let him speak as the oracles of God. If anyone ministers, let him do it as with the ability which God supplies, that in all things God may be glorified through Jesus Christ, to whom belong the glory and the dominion forever and ever. Amen (1 Peter 4:10-11).

Spiritual gifts generally fall into two categories:

1. Speaking gifts ... Which depend on an ability to communicate with the common language. Gifts such as:

teaching, evangelism, exhortation, wisdom, knowledge, and prophecy would be included in this category.

2. Serving gifts ... Which call on a person to give of themselves in ministering to others acts of service. These include gifts such as: helps, faith, giving, administration, and acts of mercy.

The biblical counselor may possess any number of, and combination of, gifts. It is imperative, however, that a speaking gift or gifts will be included. In order to warn, stimulate and encourage a person the counselor will need to be able to communicate the truth of scripture in a way people can understand. We most often find that biblical counselors possess the gifts of teaching and/or exhortation. It is especially wonderful when these gifts are combined with serving gifts such as mercy or helps but to be a biblical counselor one must be able to explain the Word in a way that encourages people to press on toward Christ-likeness.

These gifts carry with them a special responsibility to study the Word. There is a stern warning that James gives concerning teachers:

My brethren, let not many of you become teachers, knowing that we shall receive a stricter judgment (James 3:1 NKJV). Those who teach, which is what we do as counselors, must study to insure that the counsel they give is truthful. To give false counsel could bring damage to a person and the reputation of Christ. If there is not a fundamental desire to study and learn the Word of God we would not expect that person to be gifted in this way. That is not to say that our desires and disciplines do not ebb and flow but the consistent pattern of life will be to study the Word and use what you learn to help others overcome their struggles.

Gifts as passions

What would you do for free? Is there anything that you would do for the kingdom of God, whether you got paid for it or not? These are good questions to ask when seeking to discover your calling. Don't confuse passion with emotion, however. Here passion is that deep sense of what your life is about. What tugs at your heart regardless of whether you are tired or busy or otherwise distracted? If you hurt when you hear of others hurting and if you have a desire to talk them through their struggles you may very well be called to counsel. Whether you are called to fill a paid position in a church or as a "lay" counselor or visiting over a cup of tea or the back yard fence, God will reveal in due time. But if you are called you must pursue it from a pure heart, always seeking to grow in Christ-likeness through a continued study of the Bible and the application of what you learn. If you are called to counsel you will be able to do nothing else, finding no rest until you fulfill God's calling on your life.[37]

---

[37] See *Discovering the Will of God* by Sinclair Ferguson, Banner of Truth Trust, for an excellent discussion of the discovery of one's calling.

CHAPTER 8

THE CHARACTER OF THE COUNSELOR

The processes and techniques that are presented in this book are, we believe, extremely important and helpful to the counseling process. What we discuss in this chapter, however, is of a very different nature. What we look at here is the heart of the counselor. It is not enough for the counselor to be a Christian. The biblical counselor must be a person of character, in the active pursuit of Christ-likeness, and filled with compassion for those who are struggling. To understand the character of the counselor we will look briefly at two portions of Scripture, beginning with the beatitudes.[38]

The truly blessed
Jesus sat down with His disciples on a hillside one day and began to teach them and the crowds around them. What He had to say was to cut against the grain of how the Jews of the day would have thought. At a time when they viewed the righteous as those who proved to be so externally, it must have been a great shock for them to hear Jesus say: *For I say to you, that unless your righteousness exceeds the righteousness of the scribes and Pharisees, you will by no means enter the kingdom of heaven* (Matthew 5:20). What could He mean by "exceed"? Who could exceed the righteousness of the Pharisees? The ultimate answer is anyone who is righteous from the heart. As we look at the

---

[38] We are especially indebted to three men for their work on the Sermon on the Mount. We give grateful acknowledgement to their works for their influence: *Studies in the Sermon on the Mount* by D. Martyn Lloyd-Jones, Eerdman's; *Christian Counter Culture* by John Stott, InterVarsity Press; *The Sermon on the Mount* by Sinclair Ferguson, Banner of Truth Trust.

beatitudes it will become clear that if our hearts are right before God we will possess the character required for those who would speak for God.

For each of the beatitudes Jesus begins with the word "blessed". Blessed is a word full of meaning. It means to be happy, blissful or fortunate, but not simply in the subjective sense of situational happiness. It involves the objective favor of God bestowed upon the person possessing the character trait. So while it is a blessing experienced by the person it is bestowed by God on the person rightly related to God in accord with the personal possession and demonstration of the character trait.

Blessed are the poor in spirit, for theirs is the kingdom of heaven (Matthew 5:3).
- Spiritual poverty is the basis of our character. We bring to the cross nothing in our own defense. We must understand the depth of our depravity and the debt that we owe to God for saving us.
- Luke 15:11-32; Luke 14:31-33; Romans 3:10-12; Revelation 3:17
- Spiritual poverty purchases a kingdom.

Blessed are those who mourn, for they shall be comforted (Matthew 5:4).
- Out of our deep sense of spiritual poverty comes a deep mourning over our own spiritual death. We understand how sin, our own sin as well as the sin of others, has hurt the heart of God. Many people recognize that they are spiritually impoverished but it is another step to have real sorrow over that poverty.
- Romans 7:24-25; Psalm 130:1-4; Luke 4:16-21; 1 Corinthians 5:1-2

Blessed are the meek, for they shall inherit the earth (Matthew 5:5). One who mourns comes up from his knees a changed man. He has a changed heart toward God and he is changed towards others. No longer does he have a haughty attitude of being above

anyone but he seeks to pass on the grace and mercy that has been extended toward himself.
- "To be meek is to have a humble and gentle attitude to others which is determined by a true estimate of ourselves" (Lloyd-Jones). Personal humility is exhibited toward other hurting, sinful people for the purpose of helping them find the blessing they can receive from a gracious God.
- Psalm 37:8-11; Matthew 11:29; Philippians 2:5-11; Zechariah 9:9

The first three beatitudes focus on a person's standing before God. Beginning with the fourth beatitude Jesus shifts our perspective from looking inward to looking outward. The remaining beatitudes should be our response to a proper understanding of who we are.

Blessed are those who hunger and thirst for righteousness, for they shall be filled (Matthew 5:6).
- "To hunger and thirst for righteousness is to long for a right relationship to God, to desire to live rightly before him in the world and to desire to see right relationships restored in the lives of others" (Ferguson). When we experience the feast that is His righteousness we are hungry for more. As Ferguson points out, however, this righteousness is not only for ourselves but we want to see others in our world experience it as well. We are not hoarders. We want others to have what we have found in Christ.
- John 4:13-14; Psalm 119:20; Romans 5:21-22; John 7:37-39; Jeremiah 15:16

Blessed are the merciful, For they shall obtain mercy (Matthew 5:7).
- Mercy is compassion for people in need (Stott). Because we recognize the great mercy extended to us by God we cannot help but show mercy to others.
- Luke 10:30-37; Matthew 18:21-35

Blessed are the pure in heart, for they shall see God (Matthew 5:8).
- Pure in heart is the single-mindedness of those who are free from a divided self. The pure in heart avoids hypocrisy at all cost. His whole life, public and private, is transparent before God and man and there is no attempt to live a "double life". The pure heart is the undivided heart which is free from competition from other gods.
- Psalm 24:4-6; Psalm 86:11-12; Psalm 51:6,10; Matthew 23:25-28

Blessed are the peacemakers, for they shall be called sons of God (Matthew 5:9).
- Peacemaking is the cessation of hostilities between man and God. God the Father is a peacemaker between Himself and sinful people, having provided the Savior. As we seek to be peacemakers between God the Father and other people by offering to them the work of the Savior we are truly our Father's children.
- 2 Corinthians 5:16-21; Luke 17:3; Colossians 3:15; Ephesians 4:1-3

Blessed are those who are persecuted for righteousness' sake, for theirs is the kingdom of heaven (Matthew 5:10).
- Persecution is the token of genuineness (Stott). Those who follow Jesus will face persecution as the values of Christ collide with the values of the world. There will be times that counselees will not like us because we have sought to show them their sin. While we are not here to please man we are to be kind and compassionate. It is a reality, however, that some will reject us for what we believe and for what they think we believe about them. Remember, Christ has gone before us (Hebrews 4:14-16) and we must handle each rejection with humility.
- John 15:20; Luke 6:22-23; Acts 5:41; Luke 6:26; 1 Peter 4:12-19

In the beatitudes Jesus summarizes the character of the Christian and shows that such character flows from a humble heart. If the biblical counselor possesses this attitude he or she will be able to counsel in increasing measure with the proper attitude of heart and will present himself or herself to the counselee as one who has his best interest in mind.

The position of the counselor
The Apostle Paul summarizes the Christian's character as it relates to other people in Colossians 3:12-14. We will examine this passage briefly to reinforce our position in Christ and how we express our position to others.

Therefore, as God's chosen people, holy and dearly loved, clothe yourselves with compassion, kindness, humility, gentleness and patience. Bear with each other and forgive whatever grievances you may have against one another. Forgive as the Lord forgave you. And over all these virtues put on love, which binds them all together in perfect unity (Colossians 3:12-14 NIV).

• *God's chosen people*: This is a passage that talks about holy living. As one of God's chosen people the counselor must be absolutely certain that he belongs to God, that he is chosen of God, that he is part of that royal priesthood spoken of in 1 Peter 2.
• *Holy and dearly loved of the Father*: But we are more than God's chosen people, we are also **holy and dearly loved** of the Father. Holy means that we are different, we are separate from the rest of the world. We in biblical counseling should not be afraid to speak the word of truth, rightly applied, even if it goes against the tide of current theory in our secular universities and secular writings. We have to be willing to be the people of God that He means for us to be in all aspects.
• *Clothe yourselves*: Remember that when a person looks at you, they see your clothing, and this is what Paul is saying

here. Put on the following character qualities so that you appear to be the people you are supposed to be from the heart.

The expression of your position[39]

A quick overview of the following characteristics will verify that there is much overlap between the different characteristics used. We will look at their distinctives in order to form a perspective of what the Apostle Paul is teaching concerning the character of the people of God.

- *Compassion*: a very deep feeling such as Paul spoke of as a yearning with the affection of Christ (Philippians 1:8). Is this counselee just another client or have we taken the time to entreat the Lord on his or her behalf and formulate a deep desire for him or her as a brother or sister in Christ.
- *Kindness:* God is kind (Romans 2:4) and we are to be like Him. This is a goodness of heart that shows itself to be filled with compassion toward people, much like the Good Samaritan of Luke 10:25-37. Another term to describe this idea of kindness is that of caring. We must exhibit care as we deal with our counselees. Taking stock of who they are, their maturity level, and the level of diplomacy needed, given the particular person.
- *Humility*: the idea of humility is linked to the proper understanding of ourselves before God as we discussed in the first beatitude. We are not to think too highly of ourselves nor are we to play the "martyr" by speaking of ourselves in terms that do not display our understanding of our worth in Christ. Rather we are to have an accurate or sober judgment of ourselves (Romans 12:3). This allows the counselee to realize that what we have we freely offer them, and that we

---

[39] Many of the ideas for the following come from two fine works: *New Testament Commentaries: Philippians, Colossians and Philemon* by William Hendriksen, Baker Book House; *The Christian Counselor's Commentary: Galatians, Ephesians, Colossians, Philemon* by Jay E. Adams, Timeless Texts.

are not better than they although we may be more developed in maturity in a particular issue.

• *Gentleness*: Again we find a direct link to the beatitudes. The gentle or meek understand struggle. They understand the sufferings of Christ on their behalf and in humility realize that the struggle of another is ours as well, both as brother or sister or as fellow struggler. It is at this point that some biblical counselors have brought discredit upon our movement. We must agonize with people and lead them gently, with Galatians 6:1-2 in mind: *Brethren, if a man is overtaken in any trespass, you who are spiritual restore such a one in a spirit of gentleness, considering yourself lest you also be tempted. Bear one another's burdens, and so fulfill the law of Christ.*

• *Patience*: Longsuffering is a unique quality. We all want to see progress and when we approach counseling as a project or job we will be particularly susceptible to impatience. How easy it is to forget how we struggle with habitual sin ourselves. Pride may tell us that our sin is more difficult than theirs, but humility will tell us to be patient for we are not that different. Be patient. They are sinners like you are.

• *Bear with each other*: How hard it is to put up with another and yet how many problems would be avoided if we would do so. So many of the problems faced in family relationships have at the heart someone who is not bearing with someone else. The point is not that we put up with sin but it is to say that we continue to cheer on the one who is struggling. It is interesting that this particular quality comes between patience and forgiveness because they are all so closely linked. Patience requires bearing up which requires forgiveness for the need to bear up.

• *Forgive whatever grievances you may have against one another. Forgive as the Lord forgave you ...*: How did the Lord forgive? He convicted us of our sin and in the midst of our sin, He pursued us. The Lord was the offended party yet He, out of love, pursued those who were doing the offending to bring about reconciliation (Romans 5:8). At times people will come to us and show us their sin. The man or woman of God upon seeing his or her sin will quickly confess it and ask forgiveness. When we are the ones who are being asked to forgive we should be anxious to grant the forgiveness sought. This is Christ-likeness at work.

• *And over all these virtues put on love, which binds them all together in perfect unity* ...: Love is a unifying factor. It does not require anything. It is giving with no expectation of return. How this changes the counseling relationship. If we as counselors give without expecting or requiring them to love us or think we are wise or wonderful, our focus is not on self but on helping the person draw closer to Christ-likeness. That frees us from the entanglements that lead to feelings of celebrity or importance. It frees us from pride.

Seek first kingdom character?

An examination of the characteristics of a godly person should leave us convicted in those areas where we fall short, but it should encourage us in regards to what we can accomplish as ambassadors for Christ who continue steadfast to pursue Him. Jesus told us in The Sermon on the Mount to seek first His kingdom and His righteousness (Mattew 6:33). That is above all else. It is before we seek personal fulfillment. It is even before we seek our evening meal. If we are the kind of people who seek to demonstrate the character of Christ in ever increasing measure (2 Corinthians 3:18) we will be the kind of people whom those who are hurting will seek out for wise counsel. If, on the other hand, we are hypocritical or lack the depth of character God desires we may be sought out but we will do damage to the Body and reputation of Christ through inadequate counsel and a bad example. The real tragedy being that those we seek to help may not be mature enough to know that the counsel and example they are receiving is not honoring to Christ. Remember, Jesus did not say we would know the truth simply by studying hard. He said we would know the truth by following Him. Hard study is part of it but living as a disciple – developing His character – is the other part. *Then Jesus said to those Jews who believed Him, "If you abide in My word, you are My disciples indeed. And you shall know the truth, and the truth shall make you free"* (John 8:31-32).

SECTION THREE

A MODEL FOR THE COUNSELING PROCESS

THE SESSION OVERVIEW

I. The multidimensional process

The multidimensional process is based on the notion that there are many aspects to biblical counseling. The counselor should think about the process in two distinct ways:

1. The process is linear and step-by-step
Typically the counselor will keep in mind the methodology of moving systematically through the process set forth in diagram "A" below. This assures the counselor that there is structure to the process and that they are continuing to move in a focused direction. This will also give the counselee a sense that what you are doing is purposeful and well thought out.

Diagram A:
The Multidimensional Process

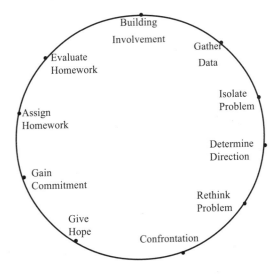

Building
Involvement

Gather
Data

Evaluate
Homework

Isolate
Problem

Assign
Homework

Determine
Direction

Gain
Commitment

Rethink
Problem

Give
Hope

Confrontation

2. The process is also variegated, fluid, interrelated, and complex. While the counselor will most often move systematically through the process illustrated in diagram "A", he will find that circumstances call him to be willing and creative enough to move in and out and back and forth among the various steps illustrated in Diagram "B" below. For example, while gathering data from a new counselee he may begin to weep when discussing painful circumstances. The counselor would want to move directly to giving hope and perhaps assign homework which would support the hope he sought to give. If at this point the counselee seems to have received hope it may be appropriate to return to the data gathering for further clarification as you seek to isolate the problem.

Diagram B:
The Sequential Process

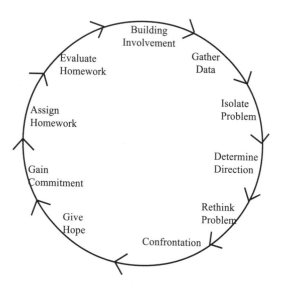

II. The Counseling Relationship

Introduction

The counseling session involves building a relationship with someone. This is important because the relationship and the process of establishing it must be undertaken in a concerted way by the biblical counselor with respect to the counselee. Through various skills and techniques, the biblical counselor can build an involvement with the counselee. In the process of establishing the relationship, the counselee is given the opportunity to state either verbally or behaviorally the potential origin of the problem with which he is struggling. The counselor also has the opportunity to provide teaching, guidance, and encouragement from God's Word on how to become more Christ-like.

1. The counselor/counselee relationship

A high priority should be given to establishing the relationship between the counselor and the counselee. While most relationships develop over months or years the counseling relationship cannot afford such a long period of time. The counselee is there because he needs guidance now. Therefore, what often takes months to establish must be established in only a few weeks.

2. Counselee reticence must be overcome

The average counselee has difficulty seeking help and guidance from a counselor, and this can hinder the establishment of the relationship between the two. In 1973, Branerman talked about why the average counselee has difficulty seeking aid. He also discussed why the counselor has to respond to this person in a way that helps establish a relationship with him. Branerman listed six reasons why the counselor should try to build involvement with the counselee.

a. It is not easy to receive help
Therefore the person coming for counseling is initially reluctant to tell the counselor the very things he needs to know to provide guidance and feedback.

b. It is difficult to commit oneself to change
Some may not be convinced they really need to change. Therefore the establishment of the relationship between the counselor and the counselee through concrete involvement is necessary to encourage the individual to decide that he genuinely needs and wants to change.

c. It is difficult to submit to the influence of a helper
This is because the offer of help might appear as a threat to the counselee's self-perception, his integrity, or his independence.

d. It is difficult to trust a relative stranger
Being willing to be open with the counselor is often frightening. In counseling this apprehension can be intensified because the counselor appears to be an ominous kind of authority figure.

e. It is difficult to see one's problems clearly at first
People have often covered their own sin so long and with so many different layers of self-deceit that it becomes difficult for them to see the problems that an objective person can quickly apprehend.

f. Sometimes problems seem too large, feel too overwhelming, or appear too unique to be shared easily with a counselor
It is only as the counselor establishes the relationship that the counselee will realize the truth of 1 Corinthians 10:13, namely, that all temptations and problems are common to people.

3. There are several fundamental skills that are necessary for a counselor to build a relationship with a counselee

a. Counselor response
In light of the previous information, one might ask how the counselor should try to respond to a person experiencing fears and doubts about entering a counseling relationship. The answer is that the counselor should attempt to understand the counselee and communicate this understanding to him in as genuine, caring, and concrete a way as possible.

b. Counselor gifts and acquired skill is necessary
The ability to communicate accurate empathy, genuineness, respect, and concreteness constitute the basic skills the counselor needs to be effective in his ministry. These skills will help him create a climate in which the counselee senses the freedom to be open, to explore his own failures, and to consider the possible ways in which the Lord might have him correct those failures.

c. Listening is not enough
Clearly, the counselor must go far beyond the simple task of listening. He has to know how to encourage the counselee as he goes through the painful experience of self-exploration and the pain of honestly wrestling with his own failures. The counselor also must be able to help the counselee move toward a resolution of his problem.

4. Accurate empathetic understanding is a skill the counselor can effectively use to establish a relationship with the counselee

a. Accurate empathetic understanding involves the ability to discriminate as well as the ability to communicate
Discrimination is the ability to get inside the thoughts of the other person — to look at the world through the counselee's frame of reference. In this way the counselor can identify with the counselee's feelings, his reactions, and the reason for those reactions.

b. A person is accurately empathetic if he can communicate
The counselor must communicate to the counselee his

understanding of the counselee's problems and struggles in a way that is genuine. The counselee should be convinced that the counselor has both picked up on his feelings and the behavior and experience that underlie those feelings. It should be kept in mind that to communicate understanding is not necessarily to give approval.

c. Accurate empathic understanding is used throughout the counseling relationship
1. Accurate empathetic understanding tends to occur more at the beginning of the counseling process because relationship building must take place at the outset. It helps the counselee to believe that the counselor is really concerned, compassionate and caring. It also creates an environment in which the counselor can successfully confront the counselee later.
2. Of course, the skill might be needed from time to time in the course of providing biblical counsel. Empathetic involvement can be permeated throughout the counseling process and help strengthen the counselor–counselee relationship.
3. Accurate empathetic understanding must not become an end in itself as in the Rogerian tradition. However, the power of true sympathy cannot be overlooked simply because the Rogerian tradition has peddled error. The biblical counselor must be able to enter the counselee's world of pain. Paul instructs us in Romans 12:15 to "rejoice with those who rejoice and weep with those who weep'. But in so entering the counselee's world the biblical counselor must not excuse sinful behavior or attitudes because of the pain of the counselee. True sympathy helps the counselee face the pain, the sin (his and others) and to take biblical action (Adams 1979). Even in cases where there is no sin on the part of the counselee, the counselor cannot allow sympathy to encourage sinful attitudes. The young couple who lost a child to some terrible disease may easily drift into bitterness toward God for "taking our baby". The biblical counselor can empathize with their pain and frustration, but at the same time teach and encourage their trust in a Sovereign, all-knowing, and loving God who has not lost control of His or their world.

5. Jesus' encounter with Nicodemus in John 3 is a biblical example of building involvement

a. Nicodemus, a Pharisee and a Jewish leader, told Jesus how he was troubled

1. In his initial remarks, Nicodemus plainly told Jesus his thoughts. Nicodemus stated he believed Jesus came from God, although Nicodemus was not sure about all the particulars surrounding this fact. The Pharisee recognized that Jesus was a genuine teacher.

2. Nicodemus came to Jesus with a question. Clearly, the Jewish leader was searching for understanding.

b. Jesus responded by declaring the necessity of the new birth (v. 3)

1. Jesus connected with Nicodemus at the point where he was most vulnerable. He understood the Pharisee's background.

2. Jesus clearly knew the heart of Nicodemus.

3. Christ's ability to be so penetrating in His discernment was amazing. The counselor usually has to look at all sorts of external visual, verbal, and behavioral clues to gradually work his way to understanding the counselee's inner thoughts, concerns, fears, and struggles.

c. Nicodemus asked how a grown person could ever be born a second time (v. 4)

1. Jesus had effectively identified the issue of tension in the life of Nicodemus.

2. Jesus' ability to identify with Nicodemus prompted the Jewish leader to dialogue further and in a more revealing way with Him.

d. Christ stated that spiritual regeneration was a prerequisite for entrance into the divine kingdom (vv. 5-8)

1. Jesus responded to Nicodemus in a personal way. It is as if Christ came alongside the Pharisee, put His arm around him, and said, "Nicodemus, I understand you have a question about spiritual matters. Let me help you pinpoint the question,

formulate it accurately for you, and help you clarify the spiritual issues that are perplexing you."

2. Jesus directly responded to the spiritual issues troubling Nicodemus. The Savior's response was accurate and balanced in its tone and emphasis.

e. Nicodemus asked how it was possible for a person to be born again (v. 9)

1. Nicodemus did not feel put off by Jesus. Rather, the Jewish leader felt drawn to engage Him further in more intimate conversation. Clearly, Nicodemus was fully open to discuss his intimate concerns with the Savior.

2. Christ had done an effective job of establishing that first level of empathetic understanding, and was immediately able to go to the second level.

f. Jesus asked how Nicodemus, a skilled Jewish teacher, could fail to grasp the concept of spiritual regeneration (vv. 10-15)

1. Having effectively established the relationship, Jesus was ready to confront Nicodemus with the truth about spiritual rebirth.

2. Confrontation was a key aspect of Jesus' interaction with Nicodemus. The Jewish leader's thoughts were out of sync with biblical truth. That is why Jesus confronted him so plainly and directly.

3. Jesus was so effective in stating and clarifying spiritual truth to Nicodemus because He had taken the time to be accurately empathetic. Nicodemus was willing to listen to and receive what Jesus said because the Savior had established a relationship with him.

CHAPTER 10

THE COUNSELING SESSION AS RELATIONSHIP BUILDING

The following is a model for the counseling session. An outline form is used with citations made in the APA style.

A. Building Involvement in Biblical Counseling

1. The counselor builds involvement with the counselee through the process of self-disclosure

a. Self-disclosure implies that the counselor is willing to be honest about himself and that he strives to be himself with people

b. The concept of self-disclosure is based on the teaching of scripture
1. In Romans 12:3, Paul urged believers not to think they are better than others. Rather, believers are to use good sense and measure themselves by the amount of faith God has given them. Looking at this verse from a biblical counseling viewpoint, we see that one needs to be accurate in his self-perception and self-appraisal. He should not be filled with pride or have an overly inflated sense of self-importance. When a biblical counselor has an accurate assessment of himself, he can relate to others without feeling threatened by others and without being intimidating to them.
2. In 1 Corinthians 2:1-4, Paul related that during his time at Corinth, he did not use big words or try to sound wise. Rather, he spoke plainly about the cross of Christ. At first, the apostle was weak and trembling with fear. Nevertheless, he simply

allowed God's Spirit to show His power in Paul's weakened condition. Looking at these verses from a biblical counseling viewpoint, we see that it is important not to try to show off to others. Counselors are not in the business of making others understand how supposedly great they are. Rather, the counselor should be humble in his demeanor and empowered by the Spirit as he exercises his spiritual gifts.

3. In 2 Corinthians 5:5-7, Paul wrote that God is the One who makes all things possible. He had given believers His Spirit to make them certain that He can do what He has promised. This truth was the foundation for the believers' cheerfulness. The Apostle also shared that believers live by faith, and this is another basis for their cheerful disposition. Looking at these verses from a biblical counseling viewpoint, we see that all believers have common problems. They also have a common destiny in union with Christ. That is why, as believers share their burdens and sorrows with one another, they can encourage each other with the truth that God has prepared them for a purpose – namely, to glorify Him by accomplishing His will.

4. In Galatians 1:6, Paul wrote how shocked he was to learn that the Galatians had so quickly turned from God. Clearly, the apostle was not afraid to be open, honest, and frank with his readers. Looking at this verse from a biblical counseling viewpoint, we see that the helper is to be open and honest about what he sees going on in the counselee's life. We also learn that there are times in a counseling session when the helper can show emotion (in this case, amazement). Doing so, of course, helps reinforce to the counselee that the counselor is genuine in his empathy.

5. In 1 Thessalonians 1:5-6, Paul wrote that when he declared the good news, it was with the power and assurance that come from the Holy Spirit, and not simply with words. The Apostle could claim that the Thessalonians knew how credible and honest he and his associates were and how they genuinely helped the

Thessalonians. In fact, when the Thessalonians accepted the gospel, they also followed the example of Christ's ambassadors through the process of self-disclosure. For example, the counselor can point out how God has been working in his life and use this information as an example of how God wants to work in the counselee's life. From this we learn that the counselor should see himself as an ambassador for Christ and an example of godliness to others.

2. The counselor builds involvement with the counselee through the process of expressing sincere concern

a. Sincere concern implies that the counselor is willing to demonstrate genuine care for people

b. The concept of sincere concern is based on the teaching of Scripture
1. Acts 20:17-19, 23 contains part of a message Paul sent to the church leaders at Ephesus. The apostle noted that all his ministry activities and experiences were fully known to the Ephesian believers. For example, he experienced persecution from unbelieving Jews. Likewise, when he preached in public and taught in the homes of the Ephesians, he did not hold back from telling them anything they needed to know to become more Christ-like. The Spirit revealed to Paul that he faced imprisonment and trouble in Jerusalem, and he openly shared this information with the church leaders at Ephesus. Looking at these verses from a biblical counseling viewpoint, we see that the counselor should sacrificially give his energy and time for the benefit of his counselees. He should concretely demonstrate to the counselee his sincere concern and compassion. The counselor should show the counselee that his primary desire is to minister to him and help him deal with his problem.

2. In Philippians 1:3-8 and 12, Paul wrote that every time he thought about his readers, he gave thanks to God for them. The Apostle noted that he regularly prayed for them and was joyful over their fruitful involvement in spreading the gospel. Paul

was confident that God would bring to completion His good work in the lives of the Philippians. The Apostle affirmed that they had a special place in his heart. This is especially evident from his statement that he longed to see them and that he cared for them in the same way Christ did. Paul later shared that his difficult circumstances had helped to spread the good news.

Looking at these verses from a biblical counseling viewpoint, we see that it is scriptural for helpers to express their sincere compassion and concern for their counselees. Part of this expression of sincere concern includes expressing joy, sharing burdens, and relating candid information.

3. In 1 Thessalonians 2:7, 8, and 11, Paul wrote that as Christ's ambassadors he and his colleagues could have demanded financial help from his readers. Instead, the ministry team related to the Thessalonians in a sacrificial, tender, and loving way. The apostle and his associates cared so much for their fellow believers that they were willing to give their lives for the sake of these new converts. In fact, Paul noted that the ministry team did everything they could for the Thessalonians. Looking at these verses from a biblical counseling viewpoint, we see that part of demonstrating genuine concern includes being gentle, self-sacrificing, and others-focused. The biblical counselor is willing to give of his time, energy, and effort in order to minister to the needs of the counselee.

3. The counselor builds involvement with the counselee through significant prayer

a. Significant prayer

Significant prayer implies that the counselor is willing to pray for the spiritual and emotional well-being of the counselee. Significant prayer also implies that truly effective biblical counsel cannot be given apart from the power of God. Adams highlights the significance of prayer. This is one of those points that the critics of biblical counseling often miss. Prayer is the first function of biblical counseling. The counselor must begin by praying for himself. Self-examination in prayer before each set of counseling sessions will help eliminate any tendency toward arrogance or judgment of the counselee. Prayer reminds the counselor of his dependence upon God. Prayer invites the power of God into the counseling routine and submits the mind to God for the direction of the Holy Spirit (see Adams, 1973).

b. The concept of significant prayer is based on the teaching of scripture
1. In Ephesians 1:15-23, Paul prayed for the spiritual well-being of the Ephesians. He indicated that he constantly prayed for his readers. Paul prayed that God would empower them with His Spirit, give them wisdom and discernment, help them to fully understand the divine will, and experience to the fullest the blessings of Christ. The apostle wanted the Ephesians to know about the power that God has made available to believers through faith in the resurrected Christ. Looking at these verses from a biblical counseling viewpoint, we see that significant prayer is indispensable to an effective biblical counseling ministry.

The helper should ask that God's love, wisdom, and power would undergird the counseling ministry. The helper also should ask that God's will be fully understood, that His power would be fully experienced, and that Christ's blessings would be thoroughly appreciated (see Adams, 1979, p. 61,62).

2. In Philippians 1:9-11, Paul wrote that he regularly prayed for his readers. The apostle asked God to increase the love of the Philippians and to help them fully know and understand how to make the right choices. It was Paul's desire that they would be pure and innocent when Christ returned. Until then, the apostle prayed that God would enable them to do good things that would bring Him glory. Looking at these verses from a biblical counseling viewpoint, we see that significant prayer means asking God to do specific and concrete things in the life of the counselee.

The helper should ask that God would bring wisdom and understanding to the counseling session and that He would enable the counselee to become more holy in his thoughts and Christ-like in his behavior. The helper can ask the Lord to give the counselee the ability to do good deeds that will result in His praise.

Clearly, through significant prayer the biblical counselor conveys his deep concern for the counselee. The counselor also demonstrates that he truly cares for the counselee and that he wants to work with the counselee to help him become more Christ-like.

3. In James 5:13-16, the writer urged his readers to deal with their problems by praying. James explained that God highly regarded the prayers of the upright and answered them.

Looking at these verses from a biblical counseling viewpoint, we see that it is scriptural to pray even in a counseling session. God will hear the prayers of upright biblical counselors. In fact, their prayers can accomplish a lot.

Prayer may occur at any point in the counseling hour. Many like to begin a session with prayer. There is one problem with this practice. It will sometimes cast a pious shadow over the session and the counselee will refrain from showing his true feelings. This hampers the data gathering. It seems best to pray with the counselee at the end of the session when the data from the session can play a significant role in the prayer. Of course, it is appropriate to pray at any time within a session when disturbing facts are revealed and/or the counselee is visibly distraught. Also, the counselor should himself pray before the counselee enters the counseling office to seek God's direction and to ask God to calm the mind and the spirit.

4. The counselor builds involvement with the counselee through projection of a solution orientation

a. Projecting a solution orientation

Projecting a solution orientation means that in the course of establishing the relationship, the counselor identifies and faces (rather than avoiding or ignoring) the counselee's problem. The counselor also proposes a systematic plan for the counselee to deal concretely with his problem. By going through this process, the counselor builds involvement in the counselee's life. The counselor does so by giving him hope for a resolution of his problem and by recommending ways the problem can be overcome.

b. There are several ways the counselor projects a solution orientation

1. The counselor projects a solution orientation by paying close attention to the problems afflicting the counselee. The counselor must be alert to the circumstances surrounding the counselee's life, the various causes and factors surrounding his problem, and the biblical way in which this problem can be dealt with. In 1 Corinthians 1:10-11, Paul urged his readers to get along with each other and not to take sides. The apostle wanted them to always try to agree in what they thought. He stressed the importance of unity because he had heard that the Corinthians had problems with factions (vv. 12-17). Here we see that Paul was solution oriented. In other words, he determined the problem, faced it squarely, and worked to resolve it. In 3:1-3, Paul addressed the problem of the Corinthians acting like people of the world. Here we see that he examined the problem, discerned its true nature, and determined an appropriate solution for it. In 5:1, Paul raised the thorny problem of incest taking place within one of the families in the Corinthian church. In the following verses we read how the apostle directly faced the problem and put forward a clear-cut biblical solution to resolve it.

2. The counselor projects a solution orientation by not ignoring the problem. If the counselor sees that there is a real problem in the counselee's life, he needs to directly and forthrightly deal with it while maintaining an attitude of humility, love, and sensitivity. There are several passages that show this process:

• In Galatians 5:7, Paul noted (rather than ignored) how the Galatians had deviated from the way of faith. Instead of avoiding the issue, the apostle dealt directly with it. In 6:1, he advised his readers not to ignore the issue of someone being trapped in sin. The apostle put forward a biblical solution to the problem

– the leaders of the church were to gently lead the individual back to the right path.

• In Philippians 4:2-3, Paul directly dealt with an interpersonal problem between two Christian women named Euodia and Syntyche. The apostle urged them to stop arguing with each other. In fact, Paul asked his "true companion" to help them get along better.

• In 1 Thessalonians 4:1-3, Paul directly faced (rather than avoided) a problem within the lives of his readers. The apostle urged them to live in accordance with the biblical teaching they had received. For example, he reminded them of the importance of being holy, rather than immoral, in matters of sex.

• In 2 Thessalonians 3:6, Paul chose to face a problem, rather than ignore it. He was solution-oriented in his counsel. The apostle urged the Thessalonians not to have anything to do with any believer who loafed around and refused to obey the apostolic teaching they had received.

3. The counselor projects a solution orientation by being balanced and measured in his approach. It is imperative that the counselor goes directly at the problem in the counselee's life. But the counselor cannot rush things. He must first establish rapport with the counselee. He then must go through the process of discerning the nature of the counselee's problem and elaborating on its specifics. Throughout the process, the counselor should remain sensitive and even-handed in the way he deals with the problem in the counselee's life. It is ill advised for the counselor to try to rush to solve the counselee's problem. Certain steps are involved in which the counselor establishes a relationship with the counselee, gets to know him, and wins his confidence. The degree to which the counselor knows the counselee and to which the counselee is comfortable with the counselor should affect the pace that the counselor sets in trying to resolve the issue being addressed.

4. The counselor projects a solution orientation by giving specific direction to the counselee about how to deal concretely with the problem he's facing. The counselor seeks to be clear and precise in the advice he presents to the counselee. On some occasions the counsel will have a strident tone, while on other occasions its tone will have a gentle quality. Examples of this may be found in the writings of Paul:

• In 1 Corinthians 5:3, Paul said, concerning the man guilty of incest, "I ... have already judged him who has so committed this, as though I were present." Then in verses 4-5, the apostle was rather blunt in telling the church what they ought to do to resolve this difficult problem. The leaders were to publicly discipline the offender, for he had been openly living in sin.

• In 2 Corinthians 2:5-11, Paul commented on how the church should restore the man who had been guilty of incest. The apostle urged them to forgive the repentant offender and comfort him. Paul wanted the leaders to reaffirm their love for the man and welcome him back as a fellow believer.

• In 1 Thessalonians 4:3, Paul specifically told his readers how they were to deal with the problem of sexual immorality. The apostle did not mince any words when he flatly said they were to avoid it altogether.

5. The counselor projects a solution orientation by supplying hope to the counselee. Establishing the presence of hope is an important part of the counseling process, for many counselees feel dejected and pessimistic about their problems and the possibility of overcoming them. The counselor needs to assure the counselee that his problems are solvable. It might take time for the counselor to build up the confidence of the counselee. Going through this important process helps to establish the relationship and strengthens the counselee's determination to overcome his problem.

B. The Data Gathering Process

Introduction

Part of the linear and multidimensional counseling process includes gathering data. The counselor cannot accomplish anything meaningful or concrete with respect to the counselee without first obtaining necessary and important information about the counselee, his life, and his problems. To gather the data, the counselor must listen in various ways, ask pertinent questions, take notes, obtain third-party information, and be observant to verbal and visual clues. The counselor uses the information he has obtained to evaluate and work with the counselee.

1. Data gathering is vital to the counseling process (see Adams, 1973, p. 257)

a. Pastoral tendency

Those involved in pastoral care and counseling tend to gather insufficient amounts of data before they dispense a biblical pronouncement to the counselee. Often the so-called "answers" or "solutions" the minister proposes are inappropriate to the real problems being faced by the counselee (see Adams, 1973, pp. 272-273). Ed Welch (1992, pp. 231-232) noted the following:

"Codependency has provided an important challenge to the church. It reminds us that past influences can be very powerful. Undoubtedly the church can do better at studying individuals and describing patterns and making relevant applications of biblical categories. We must realize that our ministry task is twofold: we must study people, together with the insights we glean from culture, science, and so on; and we must study the Bible more deeply. We have to know both well enough to recognize what it takes to make timeless answers relevant without trivializing and distorting the biblical message. To do that, counselors must be able to describe the unique experiences of others in a way that leads people to recognize "That's me!" Otherwise, biblical truth (regardless of how accurately it is presented) will seem irrelevant."

b. Data gathering through listening
Before accurate, biblical counsel can be dispensed, the minister or pastoral care giver must spend time listening to the counselee (see Adams, 1970, p. 87). The process of gathering important data will prove invaluable to the counselor as he tries to discern the exact nature of the counselee's problem and the biblical approach to resolve it (see Adams, 1973, p. 21). Without spending a good deal of time in data gathering in the earlier sessions of counseling, the counselor will lack a proper understanding of the life situation, the actions of the counselee in his attempts to resolve the problems, the significant other people involved in the problem, the physical implications of the counselee's health, and other important information.

The development of data-gathering skills and techniques is essential to effective counseling (see Adams, 1973, p. 293). Developing the art of note taking will aid the counselor in his effort to listen attentively and actively. Counseling notes will also help you serve the counselee by helping you confront the counselee with his own words; devise appropriate homework; review the case eight sessions later when your memory fails to recall details; refocus a case when a counselee returns six months or a year later for "fine tuning". Notes may also help you protect yourself in the case of legal action. The wise counselor will seek the advise of a knowledgeable Attorney concerning the laws in his area.

c. Data gathering helps the counselor help the counselee implement the biblical counsel he receives
The counselee will need the counselor to help him learn how to apply these new truths. The counselor who takes the time to establish a relationship with the counselee and discern the exact nature of his problem will be better able to walk the counselee through the process of accomplishing what God's Word teaches.

2. The data-gathering process is a concept grounded in the truth of scripture

Three proverbs give us good instruction in regard to gathering data:

• Proverbs 18:13 says it is foolish and embarrassing to give an answer before one listens to all the facts. Before biblical counsel can be given, the helper needs to know the nature of the person's problem, the attitude he has in the face of the dilemma, and how his situation is affecting the rest of his life.

• Proverbs 18:15 says, "the mind of the prudent acquires knowledge, and the ear of the wise seeks knowledge." The wise biblical counselor will obtain all the necessary information about the counselee and his life before prescribing a biblical course of action the counselee should take.

• Proverbs 18:17 says that a person may think he has won his case in court, until his opponent speaks. The biblical counselor who does not gather all the necessary data might misunderstand the nature of the counselee's problem and prescribe inappropriate means that should be used to resolve it.

3. Data gathering has an objective component

a. The PDI form (see Appendix 2)
The personal data inventory (PDI) sheet is a form the counselor can use to obtain basic and necessary objective information from the counselee (see Adams, 1970, pp. 271-274; Adams, 1973, pp. 433-435; Adams, 1979, pp. 75-76). It contains several essential parts to help you get at a complete inventory on the counselee.
   1. The PDI contains a section called personal identification. This part includes space for the counselee's name, birth date, address, phone numbers, age, gender, and the name of the referral

person. There is also space for the counselee's marital status, education level, employer, position, and years in that job. The number of years in the job might be suggestive of how stable the counselee is. The phone numbers give access to the counselee. The education will tell the counselor what he is dealing with in terms of the counselee's experience with life. The age of the counselee can be an important indicator of the person's maturity or lack of maturity.

2. The PDI contains a section called marriage and family. This part includes space for the name of the counselee's partner (if appropriate), the spouse's birth date, age, occupation, length of employment, phone numbers, length of data, circumstances of how the couple met and dated, and whether either of them had been previously married. There is also space for information concerning the counselee's children, a description of the counselee's relationship with his parents, the number of siblings he has, where he falls in the sibling order, whether the counselee lived with anyone other than his parents, whether his parents are still alive, and whether they live locally. The above information can indicate how stable the counselee is, what the nature of his home life is like, and how the dynamics of his family relationships affects the problems he is having. The data the counselor obtains from this section can give him nuances of insight into the life of the counselee, which in turn can help him to piece together what might be actually going on in the counselee's interpersonal relationships. For example, by looking at developmental issues, the counselor might be able to discover patterns of behavior in the counselee's life.

3. The PDI contains a section about health issues. This part includes space for a description of the counselee's health, the presence of any chronic conditions, the presence of any important illnesses, injuries, or handicaps, the date of the last medical exam, the physician's name and address, the counselee's current medications and dosages, whether the counselee ever used drugs for reasons other than medical treatment, whether

the counselee drinks alcoholic beverages and to what extent, whether the counselee drinks coffee or any other caffeine beverages and to what extent, whether the counselee smokes, whether the counselee has interpersonal problems in the job, whether the counselee ever had a severe emotional upset, whether the counselee had ever seen a psychiatrist or counselor, and whether the counselee is willing to sign a release of information form so that the counselor can write for social, psychiatric, or other medical records. There are times when medical complications or other problems can affect the emotional health of an individual. In situations such as this, until the medical issues are dealt with, the counselor will make little if any progress in other areas of the counselee's life.

4. The PDI contains a section about spiritual issues. This part includes space for the counselee's denominational preference, the church the he attends and how frequently, whether he believes in God, prays, and is a believer, whether he reads the Bible and how often, and whether there have been any recent changes in his life. The counselee's responses to the spiritual issues section can provide pertinent information about his status with God. The astute counselor will use this information to the fullest extent to encourage unsaved counselees to trust in Christ (in other words, be converted) and to motivate saved counselees to grow in Christ-likeness (in other words, develop character).

5. The PDI contains a section for women only. This part includes space for whether the counselee has any menstrual difficulties, tension, tendencies to cry, other symptoms prior to her cycle, whether her husband is willing to come to counseling, and whether he favors her coming. The women's section also has a considerable number of pointed questions that the counselee answers. The women's section furthermore has a problem checklist that the counselee goes through.

6. The PDI contains a final section of four questions. The counselee is asked to discuss what his problem might be, what

he may have done about his problem, what his expectations might be from going to counseling, and whether there might be any other information he should share with the counselor.

b. Homework as data gathering
Assigning and evaluating homework is a way for the counselor to obtain objective information from the counselee.

c. Third party data
Third party data (for example, from medical sources, family members of the counselee, friends of the counselee, co-workers of the counselee, fellow church associates of the counselee) is a way for the counselor to obtain objective information about the counselee.

d. The interview as data gathering
The interview (the formal meeting where the counselor asks the counselee specific questions) is a way for the counselor to obtain objective information from the counselee. The interview helps the counselor develop an idea of what is going on in the counselee's life. The counselor then uses the truths and principles of God's Word to help the counselee effectively deal with his problem and thereby grow in Christ-likeness.

1. The *extensive* interview approach is one way to gather objective information about the counselee. In this mode, the counselor focuses on a broad spectrum of problems, including the counselee's relationship to God, His people, his family, his friends, his co-workers. The data obtained can give the counselor a general sense of where more pinpointed delving might be necessary (see Adams, 1973, pp. 255-256).
2. The *intensive* interview approach is another way to gather objective information about the counselee. In this mode, the counselor focuses in depth on one central problem. The data obtained might have ramifications for other problem areas in the counselee's life.

4. Data gathering has a subjective component (see Adams, 1970 p. 208)

a. Halo data

Halo data is one type of subjective information the counselor should gather from the counselee. It is data obtained by nonverbal communication or body language. Halo data includes information gathered by observation and sound, and it also includes information obtained from tactile (sensory or touch) and olfactory (sense of smell) cues (see Adams, 1973, p. 257).

b. The voice print

The voice print (the counselee's tone, pitch, and flow of words) is a second type of subjective information the counselor should gather from the counselee. For example, if the counselee's words sound angry or sullen, it will be evident in the tone of his voice. If the counselee's words sound tense or tight, it will be evident in the pitch of his voice. If the counselee speaks slow or fast, this will be evident in the flow (cadence, rhythm) of the words.

c. Mining is worth the effort

Spending time on the subjective component of the data-gathering process can pay rich dividends (see Adams, 1970, pp. 209-210). The counselor might be able to tell what is at the base of the counselee's life in terms of his feelings, behaviors, and attitudes. The counselor might be able to gain some insight into how the counselee perceives life. By going to the base of the counselee's inner feelings and thoughts, the counselor can begin to unravel some unexplained aspects of the problems the counselee is experiencing (see Adams, 1973, pp. 258-259).

C. Isolating the Problem

Introduction

A main task of the biblical counselor is to isolate the counselee's problem. There are four levels of problems and solutions involved. The counselor needs to focus on what happened, when it happened, where it happened, how it happened, with whom it happened, and why it happened (what was transpiring which gave occasion to the behavior, thinking and/or attitudes).

1. The presences level primarily concerns what the counselee has felt and is feeling (see Adams, 1970, pp. 148, 200). (also see Appendix 3: "Four levels of problems and solutions")

a. The presences level is what the counselor sees and hears first from the counselee
In other words, the presences level is the level where counseling begins.

b. In most instances the presences level signifies what the counselee first tells the counselor about himself
This includes what a person displays to the counselor – for example, a constant frown or rigid muscle tone. Also included are what the counselee feels and talks about feeling – for example, being severely depressed, listless, confused, fearful, or drug dependent; likewise having poor interpersonal relationships, an inability to control anger, and suicidal tendencies.

2. The performance level focuses on what the counselee has done (see Adams, 1970, pp. 148, 200)

a. The focus
The performance level focuses on the counselee's inward and outward behavior. In other words, the performance deals with what the counselee is doing, the decisions he is making, and the courses of action he is taking.

b. The questions
At the performance level, the counselor asks what, when, how, and who questions to discover "why" a particular behavior is characteristic of the counselee.

c. Characteristics

The performance level includes a variety of troublesome behaviors, such as brooding, slander, perversion, being short tempered, overeating, slamming doors, holding grudges, being critical, clamming up, masturbation, cheating, lying.

3. The preconditioning level concerns learned patterns of behavior (see Adams, 1970, pp. 148, 200-201)

The preconditioning level deals primarily with unacceptable acquired habits and ways of acting. These would be unconscious and absorbed patterns from various influences in the counselee's life (such as the counselee's family, friends, co-workers). These unacceptable learned behavior patterns include sinful choices that have become regularized or ingrained behavior. These include chronic anger, avoidance of conflict, habitual lying, self-pity, and immorality.

4. The perception level concerns where the problem began

a. Core problem

The perception level is not a component of every problem. However, it is where the core of the counselee's problem can be frequently found. Getting to this core is vital to the counselor successfully resolving the counselee's problem.

b. Content

The perception level includes such things as the counselee's mind-set, beliefs, and established attitudes. The counselee often has made a conscious choice to adopt a certain manner of thinking and interpretation of reality (for example, this is the way life is or ought to be).

5. As the counselor works through the four levels of the counselee's problems, he should focus on developing the spiritual dimensions of the counselee's life

a. Conversion

For the unsaved counselee, the counselor should focus on evangelism. The counselor should explore the claims and work of Christ with the counselee and encourage the counselee to trust in Christ for salvation.

b. Character development

For the saved counselee, the counselor should focus on his character development. This includes helping the counselee establish a wide array of spiritual disciplines in his life (such as prayer, Bible reading, Christian service, spiritual gifts, use of talents, other orientation, etc.) as he grows in Christ-likeness.

Biblical counselors in general and Nouthetic counselors in particular agree that people have identifiable longings for such things as significance, security, and relationship. However, biblical counselors do not make satisfying these needs the fundamental problem to be addressed. They also do not make "needs fulfillment" the counselee's main motivation for taking a hard inward look at himself, because biblical counselors believe that the chief problem to be dealt with in the counselee's life is his severed relationship with God. The motivation for taking a hard inward look is to help the counselee deal honestly with sin issues, such as improper ways of thinking and acting. The goal is to help the counselee abandon his sin through repentance and faith and to grow in Christ-likeness.

6. Several examples help to illustrate the four levels of a problem at work in the lives of individuals

a. King Saul

Saul of Israel provides an illustrative biblical example of the four levels of a problem at work in the life of an individual (see 1 Sam: 9–10).

1. At the presences level, Saul was shy and felt inadequate about taking on the responsibility of governing the Israelites.

2. At the performance level, Saul hid from the crowd of people at the time his coronation was to take place.

3. At the preconditioning level, Saul may have learned to be withdrawn, insecure, and unsure of himself resulting from his family environment.

4. At the perception level, Saul evidently thought of himself as not being good enough to serve as the king of the Israelites. Saul may have believed he needed to do everything by himself and that the specter of failure was an unacceptable option.

b. Contemporary examples

Example One: A college student provides one contemporary example of the four levels of a problem at work in the life of an individual.

1. At the presences level, the college student is feeling depressed, listless, and lacking in energy for studying. His dejection and lack of motivation are the result of being unsure about what he wants to do in life. These are evident from his deadpan expressions, spiritless gaze, and disheveled attire. The student has sinned by not taking better care of himself.

2. At the performance level, the college student is doing poorly in his courses. For example, he sleeps in, goes to bed late, and fails to study for exams. The student has sinned by acting irresponsibly.

3. At the preconditioning level, the college student has learned that avoiding failure prevents him from experiencing the pain of feeling inadequate and second-rate. For example, by not studying, the student has an excuse for flunking a test. Since he did not prepare for the exam, he can claim his performance would have been better if he had studied more. Deeper probing reveals that the student's father is a salesman. The father frequently would sabotage a sale because he was afraid he could not get it. After undermining the sale, the father then would claim that if he had done this or that, he could have made the sale. Clearly, the son had learned his pattern of dealing with the possibility of failure from his father. The father had modeled an avoidance technique where he would set himself to fail. Because he had staged the situation, he had an excuse when the failure occurred. The student (and his father) had sinned by believing a lie. Rather

than be honest, he had embraced an excuse that was contrary to the truth (in other words, rationalization).

4. At the perception level, the college student was saying he could not fail because failing at anything was unacceptable. In other words, he had come to believe that it was not permissible to fall short of any goal for which he was striving to attain. The first sin of this young man was the acceptance of a lie. He chose to believe his own lie rather than believe the truth of God's Word. His second sin was setting himself up for failure and then inventing bogus reasons to excuse it. Within all of this self-trickery, the student had an underlying conviction from his conscience, the Spirit, and the Word that he was disobeying the Lord. This inner sense of guilt and uneasiness fueled his confusion, frustration, and depression. The counselor was able to help the student see that his beliefs regarding failure were foolish and contrary to the teaching of Scripture. The student began to see that he had adopted this way of thinking from his father. He realized that he had consciously embraced this sinful pattern because he loved his father and wanted to respect him as much as he had in the past.

Example Two: A medical doctor provides a second contemporary example of the four levels of a problem at work in the life of an individual.

1. At the presences level, the doctor was depressed.

2. At the performance level, the doctor had anger toward his family. He not only expressed it toward his loved ones, but also was beginning to express it in his professional practice.

3. At the preconditioning level, the doctor had learned his anger patterns from his father. Additionally, his mother had allowed him to practice the same kinds of anger patterns. In other words, the man had the anger patterns both modeled and reinforced by a sinful parenting style which allowed him to practice temper tantrums.

4. At the perception level, the doctor had rationalized that the anger was the result of his personality. He not only believed this idea but also was convinced that his anger pattern was unchangeable. He believed that this was "just the way I am".

D. Determining Direction

Introduction

Part of the counseling process involves determining the direction in which the counselee should move as he endeavors to resolve his problems. This step in the process includes deciding which of the counselee's problems to tackle first, what goals the counselee should adopt, and how he will accomplish those goals.

1. The biblical counselor should adopt a clear methodology in determining the direction the counselee should proceed in to solve his problems

Step One

The counselor should first ensure that he knows the specific problems being dealt with. Being able to ascertain this is largely dependent on the information the counselee supplies.

Step Two

The counselor should prioritize the counselee's problems, both in terms of intensity of importance and in terms of the counselee's capacity at the given moment to work on resolving a particular problem. The counselor usually will want the counselee to deal with the simpler problems first and then move to the more complex ones. The counselee's success in doing so is dependent on how willing he is to deal with his problems and how speedily he wants to work through them to resolution.

Step Three

The counselor should formulate some clear, specific, concrete, and realistic steps and goals for the counselee to achieve. In other words, the counselor should determine how the counselee should work through the difficult issues and grow in Christ-likeness. The goals of biblical counseling are not negotiated as they are in secular counseling. In biblical counseling goals are determined through the use of the Bible as the counselee's problems are set in its context. Such goals inspire confidence in the counselee. He is going to move in a direction which God has ordained. Since God promises the Christian to enable him to do what

God has commanded, the counselee comes to believe that he can make changes in his life which will effect the achievement of the biblical goals (see Adams, 1973, pp. 233ff). It is important to understand that the biblical counselor must work through the process with the counselee to ensure that the godly goals of counseling have been owned by the counselee (see also the discussion under *Gaining Commitment*).

2. After determining direction, the habituation process of the counselee must be altered through reprogramming, as ungodly patterns of thinking and acting are replaced with biblical patterns of thinking and acting

a. The concept of habituation is biblically based

It should be understood that biblical counseling is not a Bible-based form of Skinnerian behaviorism. The fact that Skinner (and other behaviorists) learned by observation to understand many dimensions of the God-given ability for habituation does not mean, therefore, that a biblical counselor is a behaviorist if he deals with behavior from a biblical and theological framework. It should also be understood that when biblical counselors discuss behavior they are including both mental and emotional patterns.

1. Proverbs 19:19 says that a person who is always getting angry will pay the penalty for it. If someone tries to help him, the concerned individual will have to do it again and again. The reason is that the anger pattern has been ingrained in his life. The habit capacity itself is neutral. However, since man is born a sinner, he programs this capacity from his earliest days with sinful patterns. These patterns develop into various kinds of barriers which man must confront in his growth in Christ. The child who learns early that anger can be used to get his own way develops a pattern of habituated anger responses whenever his will is frustrated by those around him. At some point in his or her life, this pattern must be broken and replaced with a godly habituated response to frustration.

2. Jeremiah 13:23 rhetorically asks whether an Ethiopian can change the color of his skin, or a leopard the color of his spots. The obvious answer was no. Likewise, the incorrigible

inhabitants of Judah, who were accustomed to doing evil, could not change their wicked ways. Their evil ways were an established pattern in their lives.

3. In 1 Corinthians 8:7, Paul wrote that some immature believers, before trusting in Christ, had habitually worshiped idols. Now, despite their saved condition, they still felt that when they ate meat, it belonged to an idol. This mind-set made them feel guilty. Their attitude toward eating meat was entrenched and not easily dislodged. It therefore was difficult for them to disassociate eating meat from idol worship.

b. The capacity for habituation is God-given

1. The Lord has given people an innate ability to formulate ingrained patterns of thinking and behaving. This ability is neither good nor bad, but can be inclined toward good or evil (see Adams, 1970, p. 150).

2. The counselor endeavors to move the counselee's capacity for habituation in a wholesome, virtuous direction. One way the counselor does this is by training the counselee to live uprightly (training in righteousness according to 2 Timothy 3:16-17).

c. The capacity of habituation is programmed by practice

1. It is through the repetitive process of thinking and acting in godly ways that the counselee will replace ungodly behaviors with Christ-like ones.

2. The Spirit can de-program the counselee's ungodly ways of thinking and acting, and replace them with godly attitudes and behaviors. Adams (1970, p. 75) observed that "though habit patterns are hard to change, change is not impossible. Nouthetic counselors regularly see patterns of 30–40 years' duration altered. What was learned can be unlearned. An old dog can learn new tricks."

3. In Ephesians 4:22-24, Paul reminded his readers that they had to give up their old way of life with all its evil habits. They had to let the Spirit change their way of thinking and acting. With the Spirit's help they could begin the process of living in a Christ-like manner, which was pleasing to God (see Adams, 1970, pp. 218-219; Adams, 1973, p. 63). Adams wrote that it is by the

power of the Spirit that the counselee is enabled to put off the old man and to put on the new man. This put-off will not be effected unless there is a complementary put-on. Furthermore, the thinking (understanding that an anger response is not only sin but it is destructive) must also be changed (see Hines, 1997, pp. 59-86).

4. In Hebrews 5:14, the writer noted that solid spiritual food is for mature believers, who have been trained to know right from wrong. In other words, they have been programmed by practice to discern good from evil.

5. In Hebrews 12:11, the writer talked about being "trained" by God's discipline to obey Him. Adams (1970, pp. 164-165) offered this scholarly note: "The Greek, like the English, mean to practice something until it becomes natural. Hebrews refers here to that kind of regular, systematic, habitual practice which makes the work of the Lord natural. Just as the athlete practices until his training makes him expert and his athletic accomplishments are "second nature" to him, so the Christian by practice must become expert in holiness, so expert that his "second nature" (wrought by the work of the Holy Spirit) is dominant, natural, and easy. As he continues to practice, the pattern is etched out more permanently, holiness becomes easier and he becomes more naturally Christian."

6. In 2 Peter 2:14, the apostle noted that spiritual frauds had a heart "trained in greed". In other words, they had programmed themselves to be selfish and covetous.

d. The capacity for habituation can be reprogrammed
The capacity for habituation can be reprogrammed in upright directions through the ministry of the Spirit and godly self-discipline (see Adams, 1970, p. 193; Adams, 1973, p. 178). Writing about this capacity Adams (1973, p. 182) observed that the only way for a person to become a godly individual is by changing pattern after pattern of his behavior from that which is sinful to that which is righteous. There must be the put-off and put-on dynamic in order to achieve a godly life. This takes what the Bible calls discipline.

1. In Isaiah 1:16-17, the Lord urged His people to become spiritually cleansed, discontinue doing wrong, and learn to live uprightly. The people were to enforce justice, defend the cause of widows and orphans, and help those in need. The phrase "learn to do good" is based on the truth that such is possible in the power of God.

2. In Romans 12:2, Paul urged his readers not to be conformed to this world, but to be transformed in their thinking by the renewing of their minds through the ministry of the Spirit and the Word. As God transformed their thinking, they would be able to discern what was His good, acceptable, and perfect will.

3. In Galatians 6:16-18, Paul wrote that believers who operate in the power of the Spirit will not fulfill the deeds of their sinful nature. The Spirit gives them the ability to say no to sin and yes to God (see Adams, 1970, p. 76).

4. In Philippians 2:13, Paul wrote that God is at work in believers "both to will and to work for His good pleasure". Both the desire and the ability to do good come from the Lord.

5. In Colossians 3:5-17, Paul contrasted the believers' old way of life with their new way of life. Before getting saved, believers were ungodly and immoral. Now, through the power of the Spirit in conjunction with the Word, the believers' thoughts, desires, and behavior are being transformed. The Lord enables them to give up their old way of life with its sordid habits and to become new people, that is, those who are holy in their attitudes and actions.

6. In Hebrews 5:14, the writer said that solid food (that is, substantive instruction from God's Word) is for spiritually mature believers, who have been trained to know right from wrong. Their discernment comes from the Spirit through the ministry of the Word.

e. Reprogramming requires coaching from the counselor until new patterns of thinking and behavior become habituated in the counselee
1. Once the counselor has determined the direction, he needs to continually coach the counselee to make the changes in his life that will promote Christ-like behavior. Coaching is necessary

because it will be hard for the counselee to change his ingrained thought and behavior patterns. The goal of promoting Christ-like behavior is foundational to the nouthetic counseling paradigm. It is premised on the belief that the counselee's relationship with God through Christ needs to be re-established through conversion and renewed through sanctification. Scripture makes the counselee's sin and separation the fundamental issue needing to be dealt with. While it is true that all people have unfulfilled needs and desires, this concern should not be the determining factor in deciding which direction the counselee should go to resolve his problems. Rather, his spiritual status before God is foremost in importance. That is why the counselor should continually coach the counselee to make the changes in his life that will promote salvation and Christ-like behavior (see Welch, 1992, p. 237).

While it is true that all people have unfulfilled needs and desires, this concern should not be the determining factor in deciding which direction the counselee should go to resolve his problems since this approach is man-centered. Rather, his spiritual status before God is foremost in importance. That is why the counselor should continually coach the counselee to make the changes in his life that will promote salvation and Christ-like behavior (see Welch, 1992, p. 237).

2. The counselor needs to coach the counselee to make specific, targeted changes. Vague, unclear recommendations from the counselor will leave the counselee feeling either confused or uncertain about what he is supposed to do (Adams, 1973).

3. The counselor needs to encourage the counselee, especially when he is feeling dejected and defeated about the difficult process of making significant changes in his thinking and behavior (see 2 Corinthians 1:3-4; 2:6-11; Galatians 6:2).

3. There are several elements or steps involved in dehabituation and rehabituation (see Adams, 1973, pp. 191-204)

Step One
The counselee must become fully aware of the nature, the frequency of occurrence, and the occasion(s) for the practice

(that is, the habitual pattern of behavior) that must be dehabituated (that is, removed).

1. The counselee must become aware of the fact that his sinful practice has become comfortable and familiar to him.

2. The counselee must become aware of the fact that he automatically responds to certain given situations (or stimuli) in an habitual way.

3. The counselee must become aware of the fact that he engages in the practice (or at least begins to do so) without conscious thought or decision.

Step Two
The counselee must discover the biblical alternative to his ungodly behavior.

1. The counselee must realize the importance of renouncing old sinful ways and embracing godly ways of thinking and acting.

2. The counselee must develop the ability to apply the truths and principles of Scripture to his specific life situation. Adams (1979, p. 37) made the following observation: "Transformation of the human life can only come through the Scriptures as the Holy Spirit uses them to effect the power of Christ in a life. This is true with regard to both justification and sanctification."

Step Three
The counselee must structure his activities, surroundings, and associations to bring about a needed change in attitude and behavior.

Step Four
The counselee must break links in the chain of his sin.

1. Changes in attitude and behavior come in stages.

2. The counselee thus needs to break down his sinful activities into their steps (or stages or links) and attempt to break the earliest link in the chain of events (or steps) associated with the sinful pattern of behavior.

3. There are at least two points at which to break the chain of sin. First, the counselee can prevent it; second, once the sin has begun, the counselee can curtail it (see James 1:13-15).

Step Five
The counselee must obtain help from others.
1. Ingrained sinful patterns of behavior are difficult to break.
2. The Lord can use other believers to help the counselee abandon his sin and embrace godliness (see Hebrews 10:24).

Step Six
The counselee must understand the centrality of his relationship to Christ.
1. It is easy for the counselee to become so focused on himself that he becomes idolatrously introspective.
2. The goal of the counselee is not just to change for the sake of change; rather, it is to honor Christ (see 2 Corinthians 3:18).

Step Seven
The counselee must practice new patterns of behavior.
1. Sinful patterns of behavior are not automatically broken; likewise, godly patterns of behavior are not automatically developed.
2. It takes time, hard work, and self-discipline to develop new patterns of godly thinking and acting (see 1 Timothy 4:7).

4. In order for the habituation process of the counselee to be successfully altered through reprogramming, the counselor must recognize the positive and negative factors that will influence and affect the outcome
a. Counselor awareness
The counselor must recognize the factors that will influence the habituation process, for these can affect how successful the counselee will be in reprogramming his thinking and behavior patterns.

b. Incremental nature of process
Often the counselee will have to take smaller, incremental steps in order to get to the larger reprogramming goal.

c. Factors for elimination
There are several factors in the habituation process that the counselor needs to eliminate in the counselee's life. Unless these factors are identified and removed, they will negatively influence the spiritual life of the counselee and his relationship with the Lord.

1. There are ungodly people in the counselee's life that he must no longer associate with. This statement is based on the truth that "bad company corrupts good morals" (1 Corinthians 15:33).

2. There are ungodly places that the counselee must no longer frequent (for example, bars, strip joints, peep shows).

3. There are ungodly practices that the counselee must no longer continue (for example, unwholesome reading, unwholesome television viewing, and unwholesome movie viewing).

d. Factors to encourage
There are several factors in the habituation process that the counselor needs to encourage in the counselee's life. The counselor's identification and promotion of these factors will positively influence the spiritual life of the counselee and his relationship with the Lord.

1.There are godly people in the counselee's life that he should continue associating with (for example, saved loved ones, friends, co-workers, church members). To help the counselee be discerning in his relationships, the counselor can have him think about the attitudes, activities, and actions that are evident in the lives of potential friends and associates.

2. There are godly places that the counselee should continue to frequent (for example, church, home fellowship groups, and so forth). The counselor should encourage the counselee to go to places that reinforce wholesome patterns of thinking and acting.

3. There are godly practices that the counselee should continue doing (for example, prayer, Bible reading, regular church attendance, witnessing, and so forth; see Adams, 1970, pp. 247-248; Adams,

1973, p. 188). The counselor should encourage the counselee to practice those things that will encourage Christ-like change in his life.

e. Reflecting on the life of Christ can help the counselor determine the proper direction the counselee should go
1. The Savior conducted Himself in an upright manner, regardless of where He went, what He did, and whom He associated with (see 2 Corinthians 5:21; Hebrews 7:26; 1 John 3:5).
2. The Savior endeavored to always obey the will of His Father. God's will was foremost in Jesus' life (see John 5:30; 6:38).
3. The Savior placed the needs of others above His own desires and needs. He came to serve and minister to others, not to gratify His wants (see Mark 10:45; John 13:1-17).

E. Reframing the problem

Introduction
Part of the counseling process involves helping the counselee to rethink his problem into biblical nomenclature. For instance, to understand a problem biblically is to have greater insight into relevant biblical principles. To address "codependency" biblically is more tenuous than to address "fear", the root of what man describes as "codependency".

1. Rethinking the problem is an integral part of the linear and multidimensional counseling process
a. Cognitive
How does the counselee put his thought processes together? Where does his process conflict with Scripture? How does his process of thinking need to change?

b. Transforming
Rethinking (or reframing) the problem involves changing the thoughts and attitudes of the counselee. This step can help the counselee move forward in becoming a more godly person.

c. Perspective

By rethinking (or reframing) the problem, the counselee has an opportunity to see his problem differently. For example, the counselor might encourage the counselee to think of the problem in view of God's providence. Adams (1979, p. 159) wrote the following: "The greatest help a counselor can bring to a counselee is to convince him of the fact that behind all suffering there is a good God who – for His own righteous purposes – has brought all this about. Having done so, he may then show him ways to enter into the blessings of suffering as Paul did."

2. The counselor needs to teach the counselee what is involved in the process of change

a. Lack of understanding

Often the counselee either does not know or understand how the change process works. Therefore, the counselor needs to teach the counselee how God brings about change in someone's life. For example, the counselor states what is involved in change, how the change takes place, and what the counselee needs to do to go successfully through the change process.

b. Three-factored process

The counselor should teach the counselee that successfully bringing about change is a three-factor process.

1. The counselee must discard old patterns of ungodly behavior.
2. The counselee must reconstruct his thinking.
3. The counselee must adopt new patterns of godly behavior.

The underlying premise is that the counselee needs to be freed from sin, for it has severed his relationship with God and others (see Isaiah 59:2). The sacrifice of Christ, the power of the Spirit, and the ministry of the Word are seen as God's provisions for helping the counselee discard old patterns of ungodly behavior, reconstruct his thinking, and adopt new patterns of godly thinking. This paradigm is quite different from that advocated by integrationists. For them the core problem is not so much sin as it is unfulfilled needs. Likewise, the integrationist counselor primarily tries to help the counselee get his needs met through Christ. The counselor encourages the counselee to "explore old wounds, to get psychological needs met, to avoid enabling and doormat behaviors, to nourish desires, and the like" (Powlison, 1992, p. 199). Welch (1992, p. 226) offered this insight: "We are certainly needy before God. But ... the needs of codependency are absolutely unrelated to being morally bankrupt and in need of grace. The codependency concept is actually much closer to "I want" or "I must have". It is not intended to lead us in submission to Christ and service to others, but to exalt our own desires. It is all an aspect of what Christopher Lasch calls, "The Culture of Narcissism, the Cult of the Self."

3. The counselor should stress to the counselee the importance of discarding old patterns of ungodly behavior

In Galatians 5:19-21 Paul listed 17 sinful acts to reflect all the ways people do evil. The representative nature of the list is made clear by his addition of "and such like" at the end. Many sinful acts did not make Paul's list, but that makes them no less reprehensible. Paul may not have intended to list the 17 sinful acts in any particular order, but they seem to fall into four categories. The list includes four vices of sensuality (adultery, fornication or sexual immorality, uncleanness or moral impurity, and lasciviousness or indecent behavior), two vices associated with pagan religions (idolatry and witchcraft or sorcery), nine vices of interpersonal conflict (hatred, variance or contentions, emulations or envious rivalry, wrath or outbursts of anger, strife or selfish ambition, seditions or resistance to authority, heresies or false doctrines, envyings, and murders), and two vices related to the misuse of alcohol (drunkenness and revelings or orgies). The acts of the flesh that Paul listed are highly varied. Yet they are all alike in arousing God's indignation.

So Paul warned his readers about the consequences of these acts. As the apostle had told the Galatians earlier when he was with them, no one who did these evil acts would share in the blessings of God's kingdom (Galatians 5:21). Paul did not mean that every believer who commits a sin is prevented from inheriting God's kingdom. Rather, the apostle meant that people who continually or habitually commit these wrongful acts thereby reveal that they are not following Christ and have no place in His kingdom. Nevertheless, believers can learn from Paul's warning how seriously God views human sin. In Ephesians 4:22, Paul directed his readers to renounce their former way of life. They were to lay aside the old human nature which, deluded by its desires, was in the process of decay. In Colossians 3:5-7, Paul uses a stronger image when he urges his readers to put to death those parts of their existence that belonged to earth – fornication, indecency, lust, evil desires, and the ruthless greed that was equivalent to idolatry. They also were to be done with rage, harshness, malice, slander, and filthy talk.

4. The counselor should stress to the counselee the importance of reconstructing his thinking

The following three passages of Scripture leave no room for doubt:

• Proverbs 23:7: the writer says, "as he thinks within himself, so he is." In other words, the way a person thinks will affect the way he acts.

• Matthew 12:34-35: Jesus declared that good people bring good things out of their hearts (their inner attitudes, desires, and thoughts), whereas evil people bring evil things out of their hearts.

• Romans 12:1-2: Paul talked about renewing one's mind. The apostle said that in view of God's undeserved kindness, Christians were to offer their bodies as living sacrifices to Him. Paul was talking about dedicating one's heart, mind, and will in service to the Lord. Such an act of worship was to be pure and pleasing to Him. The desire to serve God was reasonable and legitimate.

As believers yield themselves to the Lord, they will no longer model their behavior after the mores of this wicked age. God wants to radically alter the desires and actions of His people so that they are characterized by virtue rather than vice. As they renounce the things of the world, their thinking will be renewed. As God renews the thinking of believers, they will be able to recognize His will for them. The Lord's desires for His people are always beneficial, eternally satisfying, and flawless. When Christians submit to God's plan for them, they will mature as believers and lead productive lives and will begin to realize that those real human needs are being satisfied. The spiritual transformation being referred to in Romans 12:2 does not take place in a single event. Instead, it is a lifelong process. It is also not a mere option for the Christian. Rather, God's people must submit to His renewing work in their lives. He brings about change through a variety of means, including prayer, the study of His Word, and Christian fellowship.

In Ephesians 4:23, Paul directed his readers to be renewed in mind and spirit. One of the ways of doing this is mentioned by Paul in Philippians 4:6-9. Paul urged his readers to pray about their concerns, rather than worry about them. They were to offer their prayers and requests to God with thankful hearts. Then, because they belonged to Christ, God would bless them with peace that no one could completely understand. This God-given peace would control the way they thought and felt. In light of these injunctions, the apostle urged the Philippians to focus their thoughts on what is true, pure, right, holy, friendly, and proper. He implored them never to stop thinking about what is genuinely worthwhile and deserving of praise. In Colossians 3:10, the apostle related that the believer's new nature was constantly being renewed in the image of its Creator and brought to a greater knowledge of God.

5. The counselor should stress to the counselee the importance of adopting new patterns of godly behavior

The following Bible passages certainly leave no doubt that such action is essential to resolving a variety of human problems:

* Romans 6:13
Paul wrote that we are not to offer the parts of our body to sin as instruments of wickedness. Rather, we are to offer our total selves to God with our bodily capacities "as instruments of righteousness". The apostle noted that God's plan for His people is that they will not let sin continue to rule their lives, for they are now ruled by God's grace, not the law (v. 14). Under grace the believer has the freedom to live according to a higher principle – namely, a principle that is rooted in the resurrection life of Christ.

* Romans 12:9-21
Paul described how believers, who have been renewed in their thinking, should act. For example, if one's compassion for others is filled with pretense, it does not come from the Lord. Christ-like love is sincere and virtuous. On the one hand, it holds tight to all that is good. On the other hand, Christ-like compassion loathes whatever is not of the Lord (v. 11). Verse 12 contains four exhortations that are vital to one's walk with Christ:

First, our hope of redemption in Christ should keep us joyful despite the hardships we experience.

Second, we are to remain patient when we experience hardship. Third, we should keep praying in good times and bad times. Verse 13 reminds us that we should do what we can to take care of God's hurting people. We should also extend hospitality to traveling Christians. This should not be a one-time event, but rather a lifelong practice. In verses 14-16, Paul told his readers how they should respond to friends, neighbors, and enemies of the gospel. We should ask the Lord to bless those who mistreat us. When others rejoice over the good things happening in their life, we should rejoice with them. When others grieve over some tragedy they have experienced, we should grieve with them.

Finally, we should promote harmony and unity, not discord and division. Paul said God's people should not be swayed by one's social standing. Christians should willingly associate with others, regardless of their economic status (v. 18).

Believers should also freely give themselves to humble, or menial, tasks. Paul's comments are summed up in Leviticus 19:18, "love your neighbor as yourself". Paul's exhortations in Romans 12:17-21 concern how believers should relate to those who are hostile to them. He began by saying that believers should never mistreat someone who has mistreated them. The Christians at Rome were to consider what was noble and virtuous in the sight of all people and focus on doing that. Jesus' followers were to use whatever means were at their disposal to promote harmony. Paul urged his friends not to get even when others abused and exploited them. Instead, Christians were to wait for God to right all injustices in His time (Romans 12:19; see Deuteronomy 32:35). Believers should give their enemies food to eat and liquid to drink (Romans 12:20; see Proverbs 25:21-22). In this way, Christians might bring them to repentance. Paul concluded by exhorting his readers to resist the desire to counter-attack their opponents. Instead, the believers at Rome were to defeat evil by doing good (Romans 12:21).

• Galatians 5:22-23
Paul presented a list of godly virtues produced by those who yield their life to the Spirit. This list is representative, rather than exhaustive. The items mentioned are some of the effects appearing in the lives of those in whom the Spirit of God dwells. Paul used a singular word for "fruit". He could have said "fruits", but he did not. He may have wanted to suggest that the aspects of the fruit of the Spirit develop and grow together like a bunch of grapes. They are not separate pieces of fruit existing independently of each other. All the elements of the fruit of the Spirit should be found in all believers. Love is at the top of Paul's list of spiritual fruit because all the other virtues develop from it. Love is the opposite of the selfishness of the flesh. Joy and peace follow. Paul then listed long-suffering (or patience), gentleness, goodness, faith (or faithfulness), meekness, and temperance (or self-control). The law contained a curse against those who failed to keep it. But, for two reasons, that curse does not apply to those who are bearing the fruit of the Spirit. First,

Christ has fulfilled the law for them. Second, they are fulfilling the law through the bearing of the fruit of the Spirit.

• Ephesians 4:24
Paul directed his readers to put on the new nature, which was created in God's holy likeness. Such a new nature showed itself in the upright and devout life enjoined by the truth of Scripture.

• Ephesians 4:25
The apostle urged his readers to stop lying and to start telling the truth. They were to discontinue getting so angry that they sinned. Paul urged his readers to be honest, hard workers, not thieves. They were to replace dirty talk with wholesome, edifying conversation. Rather than lash out in anger, they were to be kind, merciful, and forgiving.

• Colossians 3:9-10
Paul urged his readers to put on the new nature, having discarded the old human nature. The character, thoughts, aspirations, and activities of the new nature are described in verses 12-17. Such virtues as love, humility, godliness, and patience were inseparably part of the believer's new nature.

• 2 Timothy 2:22-24
Paul gave his beloved co-worker some prudent counsel. The apostle wrote that in order for Timothy to be set apart for noble or godly tasks, he had to shun temptations in which young people loved to indulge themselves. Paul's co-worker also had to pursue such godly virtues as justice or uprightness, faith or integrity, love, and peace. He was to do so along with those who trusted and worshiped the Lord in singleness of mind and purity of heart. As a faithful minister of the gospel, Timothy was to disassociate himself from foolish and senseless controversies, for these led to arguments and fights within the church. As a servant of the Lord, Timothy was to have nothing to do with quarrels. Instead, he was to gently treat others, aptly teach them the truth, remain patient and forgiving when wronged, and humbly correct those who opposed the gospel.

6. The counselor needs to teach the counselee how to rethink his problem through the implementation of biblical principles

This is done with an awareness of and sensitivity to the counselee's current situation.

1. The counselor should encourage the counselee to go to God in prayer and bring Him their requests. They also were to consider how He who is all-powerful, all-knowing, and ever-present could handle their problems.

2. The counselor should encourage the counselee to replace his anxiety over his problems with the peace of God. For example, Paul told the Philippians that the inner tranquility of mind that the Lord produces is incomprehensible. His peace also transcends the worst circumstances of life.

3. The counselor should encourage the counselee to adopt a proper attitude about God, humanity, and life. For example, Paul urged the Philippians to meditate on ideas and thoughts that are wholesome, pure, upright, and honorable. Doing this would help them uproot ungodly thought patterns and replace them with godly ones.

4. The counselor should encourage the counselee to put into practice the biblical truths and principles he has learned and will learn in the future. (This statement reflects what Paul said to the Philippians.) As the counselee heeds the teachings of Scripture, the God of peace will be with him throughout all his ordeals.

7. There are three key steps the counselor should follow to help the counselee implement the biblical principles he has learned

1. The counselor should help the counselee analyze the nature of his problem. The counselor might suggest that the counselee keep a diary or journal in which he describes the problem he is facing, when he encounters it, what he thinks and feels when the problem arises, and how he has tried to deal with the issue.

2. The counselor should help the counselee identify ungodly patterns of thinking and behaving that might be recorded in his diary or journal.

3. The counselor should help the counselee formulate a strategy or plan for implementing biblical principles that will help him successfully deal with and overcome his problem.

8. There are five key truths the counselor should help the counselee remember as he rethinks his problem and applies the truths of God's Word to his life

1. The counselor needs to stress the importance of the counselee remaining honest in his assessment about the nature of his problem and his ability to resolve it. In Romans 12:3, Paul noted that people of the world are characterized by haughtiness. Christians, however, are to be humble. By the authority of the grace the Lord had given him, Paul directed the believers at Rome not to have an inflated opinion of themselves or their importance in the church. Instead, they were to form a sober and sensible estimate of their abilities based on the amount of faith God had given them.

2. The counselor needs to stress the importance of the counselee tackling and resolving his problems in the power of the Spirit. In Ephesians 5:18, Paul urged his readers to "be filled with the Spirit". This means they were to allow the Spirit to control and direct their lives. Only the Spirit can enable the counselee to successfully overcome his problems.

3. The counselor needs to stress the importance of the counselee remaining united to Christ by faith. In John 15:4, Christ taught that only those who remain united to Him by faith would bear spiritual fruit. In fact, as verse 6 makes clear, apart from Christ the believer can do nothing. From this truth it is evident that the counselee's union with Christ is the key to his overcoming his problems successfully.

4. The counselor needs to stress to the counselee that as a believer, he is dead to the power of sin and alive to the transforming power of God. This is the truth Paul developed in Romans 6:1-14. The apostle noted that all believers have been identified with Christ's death, burial, and resurrection. Consequently, they were no longer slaves to sin; rather, they were servants of the Lord.

5. The counselor needs to stress the importance of the counselee bringing glory to God as he successfully overcomes his problems (Adams, 1970, pp. 54-55). As Paul wrote in 1 Corinthians 10:31, "Whether, then, you eat or drink or whatever you do, do all for the glory of God." Peter likewise declared in 1 Peter 4:11 that in whatever believers did God was to be glorified.

F. Confronting the Counselee

Introduction
The counselee will not begin to sincerely and forthrightly deal with his problem until the counselor urges him to do so. In confronting the counselee, the counselor goes through the difficult but necessary task of holding him accountable for his present situation and for resolving it through the power and wisdom of God.

1. Both secular psychologists and biblical counselors acknowledge the viability of confrontation in the counseling process
a. Gerard Egan
In his book entitled *The Skilled Helper* (1985), Gerard Egan presented information on the importance of confrontation in counseling. Egan noted interpersonal confrontation occurs regularly in everyday life as well as in professional helping relationships. Egan presented a list of counseling professionals who have advocated confrontation as a methodology.

Confrontation has been the topic of a certain minimal amount of research (Egan, 1985). Some research has concluded that it is useful. Some research found evidence as to the ineffective nature of confrontation. Furthermore, to add to the confusion in the secular community, there is not a standard definition for confrontation. When reading secular references which favor the use of confrontation, the student is left with the question of the purpose of confrontation in counseling. Egan answers this question saying, "...it depends." He then discusses the nature and goals of confrontation in order to help the beginner decide if and when he should use this skill. Egan, after some lengthy discussion, concludes that confrontation is a valuable tool for the "unmasking of the discrepancies, distortions, games, and smoke-screens the client uses to hide both from self-understanding and from constructive behavioral change".

b. Eugene Kennedy

In 1977 Eugene Kennedy wrote a book entitled *On Becoming a Counselor: A Basic Guide for Non-Professional Counselors*. Writing about the use of confrontation Kennedy tells us that confrontation represents an intervention on the part of the counselor in order to get the client to face the realities of his situation. Ordinarily, confrontation aims at exposing the client's defenses or the defective pattern of behavior that the client employs to adjust to life. A counselor aims at interpreting the client's behavior attitudes through this and hopes to bring the client to a greater insight and self-understanding.

For Kennedy the confrontation pivots on the client's style as it is reflected in the counselor relationship. It is quite common for the well-educated bright clients to avoid the tender spots of their psyches by using the defense mechanism termed "intellectualization". The essence of this defense consists in being able to abstract one's problem and talk about it in the theoretical. If the counseling is to move into more personal material in a constructive way, the counselor may have to point out the way in which the client employs these intellectual defenses. Counselors do not do this by saying something like, "Do you realize you are intellectualizing defenses against telling the truth about yourself?" That would be a response in kind. More appropriate is the genuine response that reflects the counselor's own experience in this particular relationship. The counselor may for example say, "We seem to talk on and on, but we don't seem to be getting very far." Or, "I hear what you're saying, but I don't get any sense that you're involved in the process." The confrontation that is called for here is one that builds an understanding on what lies behind the client's irritation   or tries to understand the fearful person who finds it so difficult to talk about the source of his or her own anxiety. We respond, then, to the person rather than the defensive attack. Confrontation is not designed to attack the defenses of the other person. It is employed to point out the defenses, not necessarily to destroy them. But they help the counselee to come to the place where he can set them aside.

Confrontation is not, in other words, a hit-and-run operation. It is a process involving two persons which must be integrated into the flow of counseling. The counselor sticks with the person in helping him or her take the next step in self-discovery. Counselors who have some sense of the kind of persons with whom they work will be able to develop a better sense of timing as well as a more effective style of confrontation.

c. Jay Adams

In *Competent to Counsel* (1970), Jay Adams discussed the concept of nouthetic confrontation. He tells his own testimony. The more confrontive he became the more he noted that counselees were willing to acknowledge their sin, repent, and change their behavior. "I could not help but notice that the more directive I became (simply telling counselees what God required of them), the more people were helped. Spelling out and getting commitments to biblical patterns of behavior after an acknowledgment of and repentance for sin seemed to bring relief and results." Adams writes on pages 41-42: "First, whatever nouthetic activity may be, it is clear that the New Testament assumes that all Christians, not simply ministers of the Gospel, should engage in it. In Colossians 3:16, Paul urged: Let the word of Christ richly dwell within you, with all wisdom teaching and [for the moment we shall simply transliterate the next word] confronting one another nouthetically...." Adams then goes on to make two significant observations. "First, it is a fact that God expects all of his people to participate in the practice of confronting one another..." and second he points out that those in ministry are, in particular, responsible for this ministry of confrontation. It must be noted that when a biblical counselor confronts it is not on his own authority but on the authority of God's Word.

2. Confrontation is an important aspect of the biblical counseling process for two reasons

a. God calls His people to perform nouthetic confrontation

This is His methodology to pointedly address the spiritual and emotional problems of people. God is in the business of confronting people all the time. Adams (1970, p. 41) leaves no room for those in ministry to withdraw from this responsibility. He cites Romans 15:14 and Colossians 3:16 as representative Scriptures undergirding this fact. Frey (1997) wisely refers to this nouthetic confrontation as Redemptive Confrontation.

b. Confrontation is appropriate and effective

Confrontation is appropriate in the biblical counseling process, for people are prone to dodge, ignore, and deny their sin (see Genesis 3:8-13). People try to evade the ungodly issues in their lives by rationalizing, intellectualizing, blame-shifting, projecting, and so forth. Adams (1970, p. xvii) did a review of the Moral Model of responsibility proposed by O. Hobart Mowrer (1961). In this review Adams points out that Mowrer saw the "patient's" problems as moral and not medical. The counselee suffers from real guilt, not just guilt feelings (or what is sometimes referred to as false guilt). Therefore Mowrer saw the basic problem as behavioral and not emotional. It is the violation of conscience, not victimization by conscience, which is the source of the problem and the only relief comes in the confession of "sin" and the change of behavior. Ventilation only increases the guilt. It does not relieve it.

3. Confrontation endeavors to help the counselee recognize and deal with the sinful issues and problems in his life (see Adams, 1970, pp. 54-55)

a. Confrontation reveals the sin nature

The biblical counselor is to help the counselee see that his sin nature is a root cause of the ungodly aspects of his life. As the counselor deals with the counselee, the sins of the latter should not be minimized. Adams (1970, p. 112) noted that counselees must take sin seriously since it is an offense toward God and not just a breaking of his own moral code, as in the case of Mowrer.

b. Confrontation seeks to help the counselee view his problems from a biblical perspective
Paul makes it clear in Galatians 6 that when we approach another about sin we must do so with an agenda to help them see their problem as God does.

c. Confrontation links acknowledgment with solutions
Confrontation endeavors to help the counselee resolve his problems in accordance with the teaching of Scripture and in the power of the Spirit. In other words, God's inspired Word is the standard for analysis and recommended behavioral and attitudinal change. This viewpoint stands in sharp contrast to integrationist thinkers. They believe the theories and findings of psychology, and not the Bible, contain relevant and needed truth for understanding, treating, and transforming needy, wounded, and victimized people. Powlison (1992) points out that the focal point for the integrationists is psychology. However, for the biblical counselor the focus has to be the "depsychologizing" of the church. It is the sufficiency of Scripture that is the central issue. Powlison reiterates this point in a later volume (Hindson and Eyrich, 1997).

4. There are three elements to confrontation
a. Confrontation presupposes that there is something wrong with the counselee's behavior, thinking, or attitudes that needs to be confronted
1. The issue might be some problem, sin, obstruction, or difficulty that God wants changed in the counselee's life.
2. In light of the above, the fundamental purpose of confrontation is to bring about a change in the personality and behavior of the counselee.

b. Confrontation presupposes that the counselee's problems can be solved by means of interpersonal interaction between the counselor and counselee and God and the counselee (see Galatians 6:1-2 and 1 Thessalonians 5:16-22)

1. Biblical counseling maintains that through person-to-person verbal confrontation the counselor may be able to bring about a change in the behavior, thinking and attitudes, and thereby effect Christian character change in the counselee.

2. The counselor seeks to change the counselee's patterns of behavior so that they conform to biblical standards. This is accomplished through the use of God's Word, and is made effectual by the power of the Spirit. This position of biblical counseling contrasts sharply with secular approaches that maintain that the standard for analysis and behavioral change is the counselee, society at large, or in some cases the counselor. Such standards, of course, are subjective, relative, and most often, contrary to the teaching of Scripture.

3. In biblical counseling, the helper does not spend inordinate amounts of time exploring the counselee's past. Rather, the helper discusses what the counselee has done and what he should do to rectify his problem. The reason for not delving excessively into "why" issues is that humanity's sinful bent is the underlying cause for all ungodly thoughts and behaviors. An undue focus on potential "why" issues might result in unhelpful speculation and blame-shifting. Nonetheless, biblical counseling indicates that the counselee must take responsibility for resolving the past. Even victims have responsibility, though not for what was perpetrated upon them, but for their thinking, attitudes and resultant behaviors. Quite often forgiveness and trusting God with vengeance in His timing are essential in such cases (see Hines pp. 17-32; 103-116).

c. Biblical confrontation presupposes that verbal correction is intended to benefit the counselee (see 1 Corinthians 4:14)

1. Through the confrontation process, the counselor maintains a tender and loving concern for the counselee. This is illustrated by the loving concern of a parent for her child (see 1 Thessalonians 2:7-8).

2. The counselor uses the verbal communication of God's Word, in conjunction with the power of the Spirit, to help the counselee recognize and acknowledge his problems, repent of his sin, and embrace biblical standards of thinking and acting (see Colossians 1:28).

5. Nouthetic confrontation makes explicit use of scripture to bring about a change in the character, attitudes, thoughts, and actions of the counselee

Even Adams, who is often accused by his critics of being a Christian behaviorist, writes very plainly that change must be addressed in thoughts as well as behavior (Adams, 1970, pp. 50-52).

a. In 2 Timothy 3:16-17, Paul underscored the centrality of God's word to minister to the needs of others

1. When Paul wrote 2 Timothy, the books of the Old Testament were the Scriptures used by the Church. At that time, the New Testament did not exist as an authoritative and finalized collection of sacred writings, although some, including the writings of Paul (2 Peter 3:15-16), were already recognised as Scripture. In fact, some of the New Testament books were probably not yet penned. Even though this is the case, what the apostle said about the origin and inerrancy of the Old Testament would equally apply to the New Testament. In other words, both Old and New Testaments are the inspired and infallible Word of God.

2. Paul declared that all Scripture is given by inspiration of God (2 Timothy 3:16). The apostle used a Greek term that means "God-breathed"; in other words, the Lord is the origin and ultimate author of Scripture. Although He supernaturally directed the biblical writers, He did not override their intelligence, individuality, literary style, personal feelings, or any other human factor. Nevertheless, God's own complete and coherent message to humankind was recorded with perfect accuracy.

3. Inspiration extends equally and absolutely to all portions of Scripture. All the books of the Bible are error-free in what

they teach. This involves every aspect of them. It is not restricted to moral and religious truths but even extends to the statement of facts. This includes information of a scientific, historic, or geographic nature. It not only encompasses details of vital importance to Christian belief but also anything that the sacred writers affirmed to be true.

4. As Paul talked about the origin and authority of Scripture, he stated that the study and application of it was eternally beneficial. For example, it was immeasurably useful for teaching sound doctrine and for showing people where they had strayed from the truth. The Bible was also useful for correcting sinful behavior and for training people how to live in an upright manner.

5. From 2 Timothy 3:16 we learn that God's Word is supremely authoritative. This means it possesses the absolute right to define what we should believe and how we are to behave. When Scripture is consistently heeded, God's servants will be thoroughly prepared and equipped to do every kind of good work for His glory (v. 17).

6. Thus, there is no substitute for Scripture when it comes to combatting false teaching, learning the ways of the Lord, and ministering for Him. We insult God, deceive ourselves, and cheat others when we fail to study the Bible diligently and obey it wholeheartedly. If each of us fills our lives to overflowing with God's Word, the spiritual benefits from this act will spill over to a world that needs the knowledge of salvation. There is no other infallible beacon to guide people to an eternally safe harbor.

b. In 2 Timothy 4:1-2, Paul underscored the centrality of using God's Word to minister to the needs of others

1. Paul began by summoning God the Father and the Lord Jesus as his witnesses. The apostle briefly noted that Christ would one day return, judge the living and the dead, and establish His kingdom. The comments Paul made would help Timothy to view the command he was about to receive with the utmost solemnity (v.1).

2. Among the many things Paul's longtime friend could do, none was more important than his dedication to proclaim

the gospel of Christ. Timothy was to be ready and willing at all times, regardless of whether it was the popular or unpopular thing to do. He was to use the Word to correct and censure the transgressor and exhort and encourage the wayward to do what was right. Paul's co-worker was also to exercise great patience as he carefully taught others the truths of righteousness (v. 2).

6. Biblical confrontation is accomplished in an orderly, step-by-step process

a. Data gathering views confrontation

Long before the counselor nouthetically confronts the counselee, he must gather as much data as possible. This will ensure that the counselor has all the relevant information he needs to precisely determine the nature of the counselee's problem and to accurately discern the appropriate biblical solution for resolving it.

b. Isolation of the problem views confrontation

As the counselor isolates the counselee's problem and determines the proper direction he should take to resolve it, the counselor keeps in mind the confrontational step. This is what Dr. Frey (1997) calls Comparative Silhouetting. He realizes that he needs to frame the problem and its solution from a biblical perspective in order for the confrontation to bear abundant spiritual fruit in the counselee's life.

c. Rethinking views confrontation

As the counselor helps the counselee rethink (reframe) his problem, the counselor is anticipating how this step will help prepare him and the counselee for the confrontation element in the nouthetic process.

d. Anticipated step

By the time the counselor gets to the confrontation step in the nouthetic process, he has already anticipated what needs to take place and prepared the counselee in advance. Doing these things will ensure that the confrontation step is a success. Dr. Frey (1997) has wisely dubbed biblical confrontation as Redemptive Confrontation. Redeeming the counselee from his sinful, inept, confusing and frustrating manner of life (the "old man" as Paul called it) and setting him or her upon a corrected course of life (the "new man") is what biblical confrontation is all about. It is far more than a counseling technique. It is a redemptive act.

G. Giving Hope to the Counselee
Introduction

Giving hope grows out of confrontation. When the counselee begins to come to terms with his problem and his responsibility regarding its existence and resolution, a sense of dejection and pessimism can begin to develop (see Adams, 1970, p. 140). In the midst of potential despondency on the part of the counselee, the counselor needs to assure the counselee that his problems are solvable (see Adams, 1973, pp. 39-40). It might take time for the counselor to build up the confidence of the counselee. Going through this important process helps to establish the relationship and strengthens the counselee's determination to overcome his problem (see Adams, 1970, p. 199).

1. Giving hope to the counselee is a concept based on the teaching of scripture (MacArthur, Mack, pp.189-209)
a. In Genesis 3:15

Here we find the first redemptive promise of God. The Lord declared that He would put enmity between the spiritual descendants of Satan and those who belonged to the family of God. The promise is that Jesus Christ would deal a death blow to the evil one. This veiled promise was meant to instill hope in fallen humankind that redemption was possible for those who had faith in the Lord.

b. In Deuteronomy 30:1-6

Moses announced to the Israelites that restoration would follow their time of captivity. Regardless of where their people had been exiled, God would bring them back to their homeland.

This promise would instill hope in the remnant of Judah languishing in exile in Babylon.

c. In Joshua 1:2-9
The Lord urged Joshua to be strong and courageous as he led the Israelites in conquest of Canaan. God's promises to Joshua and the Israelites were meant to instill hope as they undertook this difficult task.

d. In 2 Samuel 7:4-17
The Lord made some amazing promises to David concerning himself, his son, and his descendants. David would have an everlasting dynasty on the throne of Israel. God intended this promise to instill hope in later generations of the redeemed who would experience anguish and turmoil from their enemies.

2. Specific counseling problems require hope (Adams, 1973, pp. 41-46)
a. People with long-standing problems need hope (see John 9)

b. People with particularly difficult problems need hope (see Romans 15:4, 13)

c. People who have been exploited, misled, or abused need hope

d. People who are plagued by fears, whether real or imaginary, need hope (see Hebrews 2:15)

e. People who have experienced repeated failures and disappointments need hope (see 1 Corinthians 10:13; 1 Thessalonians 1:3)

f. People who are nearing the end of their lives need hope (see Ecclesiastes 12:1-8)

g. People who struggle with bouts of depression need hope

h. Suicidal people need hope

i. People who have suffered great loss (such as, the death of a loved one, failing health, financial ruin,) need hope (see Lamentations 3:19-24)

j. People who are without Christ need hope (see Romans 8:24; Ephesians 2:11-13; 1 Peter 2:10)

3. There are various methods the counselor can use to instill hope in the counselee (see Macarthur, Mack and Adams, 1973, pp. 46-48)

a. Refuse to minimize

The counselor can instill hope by refusing to minimize the counselee's problem (see Adams, 1970, pp.112-113). The counselor should be willing to listen to whatever the counselee has to say. The counselor should neither depreciate nor ridicule what the counselee has to say. Adams (1970, p.141) observed that by taking clients seriously the counselor facilitates the client's willingness to divulge his problems. Those who minimize contribute to the client concluding that the counselor is not really concerned and he therefore will stifle his feelings and his problems. In taking the client seriously, the counselor projects hope to the client creating a desire to solve the problem.

b. Maintain control of the session

The counselor can instill hope by maintaining control of the session (see Adams, 1970, p.168). The counselee sees that something useful and productive can be achieved by the counselor. The counselor maintains control by managing the agenda of the session. He also maintains control by regulating his emotional response, regardless of what the counselee might say or reveal about himself. The firm, steady composure of the counselor can help to moderate and rein in the counselee.

c. Establish responsibility

The counselor can instill hope by establishing responsibility. As the counselee becomes accountable to significant people in his life, it sends a signal to him and others that he is serious about himself, his relationship with others, and his relationship with God.

d. Assume a positive attitude

The counselor can instill hope by assuming a positive and constructive tone. Just as the biblical counselor knows that there is no unique problem that cannot be addressed from the Scriptures, so also he knows that there is a biblical solution to every problem. By assuming a positive and constructive tone, the counselor helps to put the counselee at ease and encourages him to be more receptive to the teaching of God's Word. Conversely, if the counselor is consistently negative and derogatory in his tone, the counselee will be less receptive and motivated to heed the truth of Scripture.

e. Don't be fooled

The counselor can instill hope by allowing neither himself nor the counselee to be fooled about the nature of the counselee's problem and the way it can be resolved (Adams, 1973, pp. 42-43). Today there is a plethora of biblical counselors who agree that those who have been told that they are sick when they are not need to understand that there is no incurable illness that is at the root of their problem. They must come to see that they are in difficulty because of their sin and the sin of others, in most instances; or else it could be some organic problem that is treatable, or some Satanic influence which they must learn to handle differently. People who have been labeled with a certain diagnosis often begin to live in accordance with the label. These counselees need a biblical understanding of the problem so that their hope can be restored.

f. Teaching about habit capacity

The counselor can instill hope by explaining and teaching about each person's habit capacity. In other words, the counselor needs to educate the counselee about the existence of ungodly ingrained patterns of thinking and acting in his life that need to be broken and replaced with godly alternatives.

g. Modeling from the lives of others

The counselor can instill hope by referring to circumstances and instances in his life and in the lives of other believers where God powerfully worked through seemingly hopeless situations. The counselee gains hope by seeing that God was able to help other believers overcome their difficulties and resolve their problems. Adams (1970) offers consideration of Christ himself, as well as centuries of His followers who have successfully faced problems such as hunger, sleeplessness, misunderstanding, hatred, discouragement. Remembering what Christ and his followers have been able to do is a source of hope for counselees today. If the counselor himself does not believe that change is possible in Christ how can he insist that every change that God requires of any Christian is possible? Age, heredity, disability, or the presence of a well-cultivated life style are not too formidable for the grace of God. The Scriptures give the needed hope, directions and goals, the Holy Spirit provides the power, and Christian discipline is the method (see Adams, p. 174 for further discussion of this idea).

h. Modeling from the counselor's life
The counselor can instill hope by being a godly role model (see Philippians 3:17; 4:9; 2 Thessalonians 3:7-9). As the counselee sees such virtues as trustworthiness, honesty, holiness, and uprightness being displayed by the counselor, he will be more inclined to want to emulate those qualities himself (see Adams, 1970, pp. 177-180; Adams, 1973, p. 168).

i. Highlighting God's promises
The counselor can instill hope by reminding the counselee of God's promises. The promises of God can become the foundation of the counselee's assurance that he can successfully make the necessary changes in his thinking and behavior (see 1 Corinthians 10:13; 2 Peter 1:3; Adams, 1973, p. 158).

Welch (1992, pp. 232-233) noted the following: God's Word discusses these influences in a context that communicates hope. The Bible tells us that past influences, no matter how severe, can never make us sin. Even in the middle of personal tragedy we have been given God's grace to avoid sinful responses when the opportunity presents itself. Our sufferings can be a catalyst for a change of focus. Instead of looking to the past, feeling condemned and defined by our childhood, persons of faith can look back to the cross where sin's guilt and tyranny were remedied. As justification is the answer to guilt and condemnation, with all the anxieties and neuroses related to Divine-human alienation, so also doctrine (e.g. the sovereignty of God) is calculated to guide us through the pressures of modern living with the confidence that there is a purpose in everything, including suffering and pain.

j. Emphasizing short duration of proposed counseling

The counselor can instill hope by establishing a moderate and manageable length to the counseling process. The counselee will experience a great sense of relief when he learns that he only needs to be in counseling two or three months, rather than two or three years. Counseling need not take long if one can lay his finger on the heart of the issue early, and if there is proper motivation on the part of the client (Adams 1970). The goal of the counselor is not to solve every problem the counselee will ever face. Rather, the counselor teaches the counselee how to deal with issues in his life from the perspective of Scripture. His problems may not be absolutely solved from the counseling process, but he will be trained and equipped to solve his problems biblically (see Adams, 1970, p. 193). Adams (1979) makes the cogent observation that the counselor should not be interested in simply helping the counselee with today's pain, but rather he should be desirous of teaching the counselee how to handle life differently so that the counselee learns how to, as it were, counsel himself when he encounters the next difficulty of life.

The following are the criteria that should be considered when determining the best time to bring a series of counseling sessions to an end:

• when prominent debilitating problems (or those that turn out to be so during counseling) have been solved biblically;
• when the counselee takes personal initiative to use the biblical principles learned in solving one set of problems to deal with other sets of problems in his life;
• when the counselee has learned what to do to avoid future failure and how to get out of failure when he does not successfully avoid it;
• when the counselee has learned how to use the Bible to solve problems that arise;
• when the counselee begins sharing what he has learned with others.

k. Gaining a commitment from the counselee
The counselor can instill hope by gaining a commitment from the counselee that he will do whatever is necessary to resolve his problem in accordance with the teaching of Scripture. The confidence and motivation of the counselee will increase when he adopts the goals proposed by the counselor. Some integrationists have asserted that the goal of counseling is to help people get their unmet needs satisfied through Christ (for example, the need for significance and security). Supposedly, the counselee will be motivated by the desire to have his unfulfilled needs met. Biblical counselors reject such a man-centered approach. Instead, they make it clear that the fundamental problem is man's alienation from God. The solution, therefore, is not getting unfulfilled needs met; rather, it is repenting from sin, trusting in Christ for salvation, and growing in holiness. Thus, the motivation for the counselee is the desire to become more Christ-like, not to have his needs met.

l. Taking the counselee seriously
The counselor can instill hope by taking the counselee seriously when he talks about his problems, sins, struggles, hurts, and pain of all kinds. In other words, believe, rather than doubt, what the counselee is saying (see Adams, 1973, p. 295).

H. Gaining a Commitment from the Counselee

Introduction
Once the biblical counselor has identified the problem and helped the counselee understand and accept the nature of his problem, then the counselor appeals to the counselee to make a commitment to do what is necessary in his life to bring about the changes God's Word requires of him (see Adams, 1970, p. 169; Adams, 1973, p. 242).

1. The idea of obtaining a commitment from the counselee is based on the teaching of Scripture

Throughout the Old Testament, God summoned His people to remain obedient to Him.

a. When Abram was 99 years old, the Lord appeared to him and said, "I am God Almighty; walk before Me, and be blameless" (Genesis 17:1).

b. When the Israelites were assembled at Mount Sinai, the Lord revealed to them the Ten Commandments, which He expected them to obey (see Exodus 20:1-17).

c. Throughout the entire book of Deuteronomy, Moses reminded the Israelites of the importance of remaining committed to the law.

d. As Joshua spoke to the Israelites who had embarked on the conquest of Canaan, he urged them to make a commitment to serve the Lord (see Joshua 24:15).

e. When the Lord appeared to Solomon in a dream, He directed the king to remain committed to His commandments (1 Kings 3:5, 14).

f. Solomon underscored the importance of revering God and heeding His commandments. Such a commitment to do God's will was necessary, for He will "bring every act to judgment, everything which is hidden, whether it is good or evil" (Ecclesiastes 12:13-14).

2. Throughout the New Testament God summoned His people to remain obedient to him

a. At the end of the Sermon on the Mount, Jesus declared that those who heeded His teachings were truly wise (see Matthew 7:24).

b. During His earthly ministry, Christ declared that those who did the will of the Father were His true spiritual brothers and sisters (see Matthew 7:48-50).

c. In Matthew 11:28-30, Christ urged everyone to "take My yoke upon you and learn from Me, for I am gentle and humble in heart".

d. Part of the disciples' great commission included teaching new converts to observe all that Jesus commanded (see Matthew 28:20).

e. Jesus declared to His disciples, "If you love Me, you will keep My commandments" (John 14:15).

f. Paul urged his readers to consider themselves to be dead to sin, but alive to God in union with Christ. The apostle also urged them not to let sin reign in their mortal bodies (in Romans 6:11-12).

g. The apostle John wrote that "this is the love of God, that we keep His commandments" (1 John 5:3).

3. All discussion in the counseling session should aim toward gaining a commitment from the counselee

a. Mere discussion of the self is not solution oriented. Counseling that is merely focused on discussion on the self does not encourage the counselee to embrace biblical solutions to his problems. That is why it is imperative for the counselor to direct the entire session toward gaining a commitment from the counselee to perform some homework or task before the next session.

b. The counselor should write out the assignment, explain it to the counselee, and seek his commitment to accomplish it by God's grace.

c. The change to which the counselee is making a commitment might involve knowledge, belief, or action. Regardless of the nature of that change, the counselor should help the counselee see why it is important and how it is founded on the teaching of Scripture.

d. It is important for counselors to help counselees reach God's solutions to their problems. That is why the counselor needs to know Scripture thoroughly and how to use it practically. Otherwise, the counselor will misinterpret and misapply God's Word to the lives of others.

4. The counselee needs to commit himself to trusting in Christ for salvation and to growing and maturing in his walk with the Lord

a. Commitment to Christ should always be foremost
Regardless of whatever else is accomplished in the sessions, the counselor should ensure that the gospel has been presented to the counselee and that he has had an opportunity to put his faith in Christ (see John 20:30-31).

b. Commitment to Christ-likeness should always be urged
In addition to the salvation of the counselee, the counselor should encourage the counselee to become more Christ-like.

1. God does not save people so that they can live for themselves. Rather, He rescues them from sin so that they might serve Him faithfully (see Ephesians 2:8-10).

2. God calls His people to live in a way that is characterized by holiness; in other words, He wants them to renounce sin and give themselves in service to Him (see 1 Thessalonians 4:3; 1 Peter 1:13-15).

5. There are three common reasons for counselee failure

a. Counselees may have a lack of knowledge. For example, they may not know what the counselor expects them to do. Or they may not know what God's Word says concerning a particular issue in their lives. Consequently, they do not know how to move forward in resolving their problem.

b. Counselees may have a lack of understanding. For example, a counselee may know what the Bible says, but he may not comprehend how to implement the truth of Scripture. In this case, the counselor needs to give the counselee instruction in methodology, that is, in how to do a particular task.

c. Counselees may have a lack of genuine commitment. This seems to occur for three reasons.

1. The counselee may lack commitment because he willfully refuses to do what Scripture says. In other words, the counselee needs to repent of his sin before he will make a commitment to obey God.

2. The counselee may lack commitment because the change in behavior enjoined by Scripture is too uncomfortable for him

to bear. In other words, the pain of the counselee's current status is less than the pain of change called for by the Bible.

3. The counselee may lack commitment because he is either frustrated or despondent about his situation. In his mind, commitment is pointless because he thinks it is impossible for him to change.

6. There are several factors that prevent a counselee from making a commitment

a. Being unregenerate

An unregenerate heart can prevent a counselee from making a commitment. The counselee is so enslaved by sin that he refuses to do what God's Word teaches.

b. Repeated failure

Repeated failure can prevent a counselee from making a commitment. The counselee may have tried over and over again to resolve his problem, but with no substantial results. He is at the point of giving up, having no hope for success.

c. Feeling orientation

A feeling orientation can prevent a counselee from making a commitment. In other words, he confuses need with desire. The counselee may desire something, but that is not necessarily a need. True, absolute biological needs (such as for food, oxygen, and water) must be met. However, desires can go unmet and not adversely affect the counselee.

1. Some counselees will not make a commitment to certain behaviors because it might prevent them from experiencing certain feelings. The counselor should explain that experiencing certain feelings is not the most important issue in their lives.

2. Some counselees who have no commitment to live uprightly will remain contented with gratifying their wanton desires. In other words, in the absence of any moral boundaries, the counselee will choose to disobey Scripture.

d. Skepticism

Unbelief, doubt, or skepticism can prevent a counselee from making a commitment. In this situation, the counselor should underscore God's power to help the counselee succeed in doing His will.

e. Lack of desire

A lack of desire can prevent a counselee from making a commitment. In other words, the counselee might intellectually acknowledge the validity of what the counselor has said, and yet be unwilling to do what he has advised.

f. Inaccurate concept of the Christian life

An inaccurate concept of the Christian life can prevent a counselee from making a commitment. A distorted view about the nature of sanctification can stifle the counselee's willingness to do what God wants.

g. Bitterness

Bitterness can prevent a counselee from making a commitment. The presence of an antagonistic or resentful attitude will hamper someone from making the changes in behavior called for by Scripture.

h. Laziness

Laziness can prevent a counselee from making a commitment. An inclination to inactivity will hinder some from putting forth the concerted effort required by God.

i. An S. O. P. (significant other person)

Ungodly advice can prevent a counselee from making a commitment. Often unbiblical counsel can confuse or sidetrack people so that they do not make the changes in behavior called for by Scripture.

j. Nonchalant attitude

A nonchalant attitude toward sin can prevent a counselee from making a commitment. Likewise, blame-shifting and rationalization can prevent a counselee from doing what God wants.

k. Excuse pattern
A pattern of excuse making can prevent a counselee from making a commitment.

7. There are several things the counselor can do to secure a commitment from the counselee
a. The counselor can assume from the counselee's attitude that he is committed to doing what God wants.

b. The counselor can ask the counselee for his commitment (see Isaiah 6:8).

c. The counselor can establish a covenant with the counselee in which he agrees to do certain things in order to bring about a change of behavior in his life (see Adams, 1970, p. 198).

d. The counselor can have the counselee objectively work through a Christian decision-making process.

I. Assigning Homework to the Counselee

Introduction
The biblical counselor assigns homework to the counselee to help him begin to deal concretely with his problem. In assigning homework, the counselor is focusing primarily on addressing the counselee's attitude and behavior.

1. There are several benefits to the counselor of assigning homework to the counselee
a. Assigning homework establishes a pattern for action and change in the counselee's life
1. Assigning homework enables the helper to structure the counseling process so that it is focused on getting the counselee to make concrete changes in his own life. This, in turn, will

bring about a transformation in his thinking and acting right from the start of the counseling process.

2. Under this approach, the responsibility for change primarily falls on the counselee, not the counselor.

3. The achievement of assignments can encourage the counselee to continue, whereas the non-achievement of assignments can encourage the counselee to make no further progress (see Hebrews 6:1).

b. Assigning homework clarifies expectations of the counselor to the counselee

1. Assigning homework helps the counselee to know exactly what it is that the counselor wants him to achieve in his life between sessions.

2. Assigning homework helps the counselee clarify for himself goals that he will establish and achieve in his own life.

3. Right at the start of the process, the counselee is required to take responsibility and ownership for the changes that need to be accomplished in his life. Adams (1973, p. 301) remarked, "From the inception of counseling, therefore, the counselee should be made to understand two facts: first, that each counseling session leads toward biblical action as its natural outcome; secondly, that he is going to be challenged to perform as God's Word requires."

4. The counselee's taking responsibility prevents him from becoming dependent on the counselor to bring about and sustain needed changes in his life (see Adams, 1973, p. 305).

c. Assigning homework eliminates the phenomena of the so-called "professional counselee"

1. The professional counselee is someone who knows the technical language and concepts associated with counseling. He usually comes to the counselor with some sort of "diagnosis" of his problem, and he is adept at using psychiatric jargon to communicate his conclusions. The professional counselee derives satisfaction from always being in the counseling process. After all, it prevents him from having to take personal responsibility for his problems. Likewise, he is

not forced to make any needed and possibly painful changes in his thinking and acting. Furthermore, he gets to enjoy the attention and sympathy his counselors lavish on him. Adams warns the counselor regarding the professional counselee. This person does not come seeking help. He comes as a way of coping with his problem rather than solving his problem. He has made a career of counseling. Often the Christian will have been to other counselors in town (see his discussion, Adams, 1973 p. 298).

2. By assigning homework, the counselor forces the professional counselee to stop playing psychological games in favor of getting down to the business of seriously dealing with his problems.

3. By assigning homework, the counselor shifts the focus of the professional counselee from himself and his problems to God and His Word.

4. By assigning homework, the counselor moves the professional counselee from merely talking about his problem to making a concerted effort to resolve it in God's power according to the teaching of His Word.

d. Assigning homework enables the counselor to gather relevant data

1. By assigning homework, the counselor obtains concrete and pertinent feedback from the counselee and other significant individuals in his life.

2. By assigning homework, the counselor can measure the counselee's progress, observe how he is responding to different situations, and discern how serious he is in making needed changes in his thinking and acting.

e. Assigning homework helps to sustain momentum between counseling sessions (see Adams, 1973, p. 238)

1. Initially, the counselor should give small, easy assignments to the counselee. This will afford him the opportunity to learn quickly how to solve problems successfully in God's way.

2. The hope gained and the principles learned through resolving smaller problems can be used by the counselee to deal with more complex ones (see Proverbs 13:12).

f. Assigning homework reduces the number of times the counselee needs to meet with the counselor
1. Assigning homework can help the counselor work more rapidly and productively with the counselee. Work is not limited to the counseling session alone; rather, it is extended throughout the time between sessions.
2. The necessity of assigning homework requires the counselor to establish goals and parameters and remain focused on achieving them.
3. The necessity of assigning homework requires the counselee to understand what is going on and become actively involved in the counseling process.

g. Assigning homework provides a solid measure for determining counselee understanding and progress
1. The counselor is able to see just how much or how little the counselee understands about the nature of his problem and what God requires him to do to solve it.
2. The counselor is able to see just how much the counselee has accomplished and changed.
3. The counselor is able to see the exact level of commitment the counselee has to do what God wants.

h. Assigning homework enables the counselor to challenge the counselee, especially when he fails to achieve the task he was given
1. There may be times when the counselee will fail to do the homework the counselor assigns. The counselee might refuse to do the assignment or might not be able to do the assignment.
2. When failure occurs because the the counselee refuses to do the assignments due to low commitment, the counselor can challenge the counselee to remove whatever obstacles to compliance exist.

i. Assigning homework provides a good starting point for the next counseling session

1. How the counselee responds to the initial homework assignment helps set the tone and direction for subsequent meetings.

2. The counselor can use the assigning, achievement, and review of homework to create and structure the process and direction of each counseling session.

3. Assigning homework can create an integrated continuity for the counseling process.

4. Assigning homework can help the counselor follow through on a specific train of thought. It also helps the counselee to narrow his focus and effectively learn how to solve a particular problem in his life.

2. There are several benefits to the counselee when the counselor assigns him homework

a. Assigning homework decreases the counselee's dependence on the counselor

1. Assigning homework right from the start gets the counselee to see that he is not just going to talk about his problem.

2. The counselee learns that he is expected to take personal responsibility for his problem and for solving it in God's power in accordance with the teaching of His Word.

b. Assigning homework builds confidence in the counselee.

1. The counselee gains confidence as he discovers God's solutions to his problems.

2. The counselee gains confidence as he learns how the Lord can work powerfully in his life to bring about needed change.

c. Assigning homework stimulates permanent biblical change in the counselee's life

This in turn forces the counselee to implement and practice the truths of God's Word (see Adams, 1970, pp. 193-194).

d. Assigning homework gives the counselee a problem-solving record (see Adams, 1970, pp. 198-199)

1. The counselee can go back and review the homework he has performed.

2. The counselee can use the information he obtains from his completed homework assignments as a resource for future reference, reflection, encouragement, and planning.

e. Assigning homework provides material for the counselee to use in helping others

1. As the counselee reflects on the changes God has brought about in his life through the accomplishment of homework assignments, he is greatly encouraged about what has taken place.

2. Convinced about what biblical counseling has done for him, he becomes motivated to help others learn how to deal with their problems in accordance with the teaching of Scripture (see 2 Timothy 2:2).

3. There are several steps to follow in constructing good homework assignments

Such homework is not only useful but also grows out of a biblical frame of reference.

a. To construct a good homework assignment, the counselor needs to ensure that it is biblical in nature

1. This statement does not mean that the actual assignment must be explicitly commanded in Scripture. Rather, the assignment is biblical in nature because it is in harmony with the teaching of Scripture. The Bible provides the framework for the assignment.

2. A good homework assignment will not only be based on God's Word but also use the Bible to measure the counselee's performance.

b. To construct a good homework assignment, the counselor needs to make the task concrete and specific in character

1. The counselor should be exacting and precise when assigning homework to the counselee.

2. The counselor's assignments should call for explicit behavioral and attitudinal changes in the counselee.

c. To construct a good homework assignment, the counselor needs to make the task practical, realistic, and relevant in orientation
1. The counselor needs to ensure that the assignment will enable the counselee to solve his problem.
2. The counselor needs to explain to the counselee how the assignment will help him make necessary changes in his life.

d. To construct a good homework assignment, the counselor needs to make the tasks flexible in organization
1. The counselor should tailor the assignment to the needs, aptitudes, and abilities of the counselee (see Adams, 1973, pp. 238-239).
2. The assignment should not be too easy or too difficult. Rather, it should be appropriate to where the counselee is at spiritually, mentally, and emotionally (see Adams, 1970, pp. 194-195; Adams, 1973, p. 236).
3. The counselor should anticipate having to negotiate the homework with the counselee. There are times when the counselor needs to discuss with the counselee about how much he is able to do and how willing he is to do it.
4. The counselor should avoid overwhelming the counselee with too much homework. Yet the counselor should assign a sufficient amount of work to effect change.

4. There are several types of homework assignments the counselor can give to the counselee
a. The counselor can have the counselee create important lists (for example: sins and failures, possible ways to quit a habit, etc.)
b. The counselor can have the counselee keep a journal or log (for example: about certain activities, about particular response patterns, about specific times when painful experiences occur, etc.)
c. The counselor can have the counselee do projects (for example: outlining a book of the Bible, responding to questions about an

article in a Christian magazine, meditating on a passage of Scripture, etc.)

d. The counselor can have the counselee "futurize"

1. To "futurize", the counselor helps the counselee talk about the present by having him engage in a dialog between a better future and an unacceptable past.

2. By "futurizing", the counselee looks at his unacceptable past, he considers the way he has been living his life, and he determines that this is not the way he wants his life to be. He then considers how he would like his life to be in the future.

3. In the dialog, the counselee tries to deliberate how he can get from where he is to where he wants to be. In other words, he ponders how he can create a better future for himself.

4. The homework assignment does not have to be cumbersome. The counselor can ask the counselee to make a simple list of those actions, thoughts, and beliefs that have contributed to the past and present situation in which he finds himself. The counselee then can consider the kind of future that would be more in line with the teaching of God's Word. The counselee should ponder what sinful behaviors and thoughts he needs to jettison and what godly actions and attitudes he needs to embrace. He should list both the steps he needs to take to achieve his goal and the beneficial consequences that will result.

e. The counselor can have the counselee set specific, concrete, and objective goals for himself

The primary goal is for him to become more Christ-like. The subsidiary goals and steps should detail how he can achieve the primary goal. There are several reasons for having the counselee do this type of homework assignment.

1. Setting goals helps focus the counselee's attention and action. In other words, the counselee is required to determine exactly where he needs to go and how he is going to get there.

2. Setting goals helps the counselee make full and better use of his energies and efforts. In other words, by going through the

goal-setting process, the counselee becomes motivated and mobilized to do what God's Word says.

3. Setting goals helps to increase the counselee's determination to become more holy in his attitudes, thoughts, and actions.

4. Setting goals helps the counselee to deliberate how he might implement strategies in his life to achieve godly outcomes.

J. Evaluating the Counselee's Homework

Introduction
The biblical counselor evaluates the homework and what the counselee did in the process of completing the outside assignment. Through the evaluation phase, the counselor can determine how serious the counselee is in dealing with the problem in his life. The counselor also can ascertain how well the counselee understood what was discussed in the previous session. The counselor furthermore can gauge the counselee's receptivity to the biblical solving process (see "Fifty Failure Factors" in Adams, 1973, pp. 459-461).

1. The counselor should ask whether the homework assignment achieved the goal he had for the counselee
a. Honest assessment
There are times when the homework assignment will achieve the counselor's goal for the counselee, and there are times when the assignment will fail to do so. The counselor should be honest and objective in his assessment of the success or failure of the homework assignment. Adams (1973, p. 343) offered this bold assertion: "Homework, then, is of the essence of good counseling." By this he simply means that homework is where the work of biblical counseling gets done. Counselors who perfect the ability to give homework will be effective in helping people. Homework, to be effective, must be biblical, concrete, and creatively applied to the situation in a timely manner.

b. *What happened here?*

To evaluate the outcome of the assignment, the counselor first should explore the question, "What happened here?" The counselor can have the counselee explain what he thought he was being asked to do. The counselor should be willing to admit any mistakes he may have made in not communicating his thoughts well to the counselee.

c. *Was the assignment clear?*

To evaluate the outcome of the assignment, the counselor should explore the question, "Was the assignment clear?" In other words, did the counselor state clearly to the counselee what he was supposed to do? (see Adams, 1973, p. 314).

d. *Did I assign too much?*

To evaluate the outcome of the assignment, the counselor should explore the question, "Was the assignment too much for the counselee to do between sessions?" (see Adams, 1973, p. 314). The counselor should remember that the assignment needs to be realistic, relevant, and achievable within the time available between the current session and the next session. The counselor should take into consideration the demands the counselee has on his time and tailor the assignment accordingly. There may be legitimate reasons why a counselee cannot do as much homework one week as the next (e.g. college finals week, a big presentation at work, etc.).

e. *Was there resistance?*

To evaluate the outcome of the assignment, the counselor should explore the question, "Did the counselee resist doing the assignment?" By asking probing and reflective questions, the counselor might be able to determine whether the counselee objected to completing the task he was given (see Adams, 1973, pp. 114-116). There are times when the counselor can use the unfinished homework to precipitate a question about why it did not get done. In the process of talking about this matter, the counselee's resistance will begin to manifest itself. The counselor then can use that resistance to motivate the counselee to complete the assignment by the next session.

f. Was the counselee motivated?

To evaluate the outcome of the assignment, the counselor should explore the question, "How motivated was the counselee about doing the task?" If the counselee satisfactorily completed the assignment, the counselor should let him know. This in turn will encourage the counselee and increase his enthusiasm in making further progress.

g. Should the assignment be repeated?

To evaluate the outcome of the assignment, the counselor should explore the question, "Does the counselee need to repeat the task?" There may be times when the counselee has only scratched the surface of an area in his life requiring further attention. By having him repeat the homework assignment (for example, keeping a journal, having a consistent time of Bible study and prayer), the counselor helps him to wrestle further with the problem and resolve it more thoroughly.

h. Have I met my responsibility?

To evaluate the outcome of the assignment, the counselor should explore the question, "Have I, as a counselor, fulfilled my responsibility in helping the counselee successfully do the assignment?" The counselor has several responsibilities. He should ensure that the instructions are clearly communicated, that the task is appropriate to the counselee's situation, that the assignment is understandable to the counselee, and that the task is appropriate to the counselee's learning style.

CHAPTER 11

EVALUATING THE COUNSELING PROCESS

1. The counselor should ask whether his counseling has been biblically based

a. A counselor can make significant progress toward making the counselee feel better and yet not give biblically based counseling

This especially is evident in the secular counseling community. There are many instances where a client who was hurting, confused, and frustrated has had his emotional "needs" met and problems addressed through the therapy he received.

b. Even counselors who are Christian or who are sympathetic to Christian values and ideas may not employ biblically based techniques

Instead, the counselor may make use of one or more secular theories in trying to help his clients deal with their problems. Because of his lack of knowledge of the Scriptural distinctives concerning the issues at hand, he may not know he is giving unbiblical advice.

c. The above observations make it clear that the determining factor cannot be simply whether the counseling has been successful in making the person feel better

In other words, just bringing about positive attitudinal and behavioral changes in the client's life does not necessarily indicate whether the counseling has been biblically based.

2. The helper should ask whether the goal of his counseling has been the sanctification of the counselee

a. Some Christians maintain that the goal of counseling is to meet "the deepest personal needs of people" (Crabb, 1975, p. 53)

In this view the counselor is to help the counselee deal with a "shattered, fragmented, fatally wounded personality". Such a view point is objectionable because it is anthropologically (or man) centered, not God-centered. The goal is not the conversion and consecration of the counselee. Rather, it is to help him perceive himself as a person having worth (Crabb, 1975, p. 53). It is asserted that such perception precedes the possibility of an enjoyable life.

This view places too much emphasis on the assumed goodness of people and meeting their unfulfilled needs, whether real or imagined. The Scriptures, however, make it clear that people have no merit in themselves. The Bible, likewise, teaches that the fundamental problems facing people are not solved by trying to meet their perceived psychological deficiencies. Rather, healing and wholeness comes by bringing them to faith in Christ. Powlison (1993, p. 29) makes the observation that all integrationist views are man-centered. Needs are the all-important dimension of man. If needs are not met, man cannot function satisfactorily. Man is fundamentally good and the difficulties of life combine with fallenness to make him a needy person. In the truly biblical scheme of thinking, effective, spiritual, and joyful living are not achieved by rebuilding a shattered and wounded personality. Likewise, the goal of the counselor is not primarily to satisfy a list of unmet personal needs in the counselee. Instead, the goal of the counselor is to underscore the counselee's alienation from God and his need to repent of his sin. The counselor seeks to bring about the conversion and consecration of the counselee. Only then can true joy and spiritual vitality be experienced.

b. The goal of conversion and consecration is grounded in Scripture

For example, in Colossians 1:28, Paul wrote that he proclaimed Christ. The apostle admonished and taught everyone with God-given wisdom. Paul's goal was that they might be "complete in Christ". The apostle wanted to see them mature in their faith and become more godly in their attitudes and actions. The biblical counselor needs to consider whether the counselee has become more mature in his walk with Christ. Has the counselee become increasingly separated from sin and more set apart for the Lord and His service? Are the counselee's thinking and behavior more godly than they were before?

c. The counselor needs to determine whether he has used a biblical methodology to promote change in the counselee's life.

If so, this will result in the counselee setting aside ungodly attitudes and actions and embracing godly ones. A Christian must start with a Christian foundation and build upon it a Christian methodology that rests upon and is consistent with that foundation. In the common grace of God, unbelievers stumble over aspects of truth in God's creation. They always distort these by their sin and from their non-Christian stance toward life. But from the vantage point of his biblical foundation the Christian counselor may take note of, evaluate, and reclaim the truth dimly reflected by the unbeliever as long as he does so in a manner consistent with biblical principles and methodologies (see Adams 1973, p. 92).

d. The counselor needs to discern whether he and the counselee have been consciously dependent on the Spirit to bring about the needed changes in the counselee's life

Only that which the Spirit brings about will be truly God-honoring and eternal in value.

e. The counselor needs to find out whether true biblical change is evident in the counselee's life

Can the counselor see whether the person has been renewed in his thinking and transformed in his actions (see Romans 12:1-2)? Is his attitude toward life, his family, his work, and his relationship with God more in agreement with the teaching of Scripture? Is the counselee operating more within a biblical frame of reference?

3. The helper should ask whether the counselee has been understood throughout the course of the counseling process

a. The counselor should ask whether he has taken the time to hear and understand the deepest concerns of the counselee

Is the counselor aware of the counselee's struggles, sins, and fears? Has the counselor discerned what brought about the counselee's problem and the things he has done to worsen it?

b. The counselor should ask whether the biblical issues have become evident

Has the counselor gathered the data and listened to the counselee share his deepest concerns? Has the counselor been able to see the real issues underlying the counselee's problems? Has the counselor been able to frame the problem and its solution from a biblical perspective?

c. The counselor should ask whether the counselee needs further biblical instruction

In other words, does he need more solid Scriptural teaching?

d. The counselor should ask whether the counselee needs further encouragement

In other words, does he need additional support and reassurance as he works through his problem in a biblical manner?

e. The counselor should ask whether the counselee needs a tutor, mentor, or discipler

In other words, does the counselee need someone to guide and instruct him further in godly living?

4. The helper should ask whether the counselee has become increasingly engaged in the counseling process

a. Is he committed to change?

The counselor should ask whether the counselee is committed to change and to what extent he is committed. In other words, is the counselee internally motivated to grow in Christ-likeness, or is his commitment primarily dependent on his relationship to the counselor?

b. Has he made the necessary effort?
The counselor should ask whether the counselee has made a personal, concerted effort to change. In other words, how much has the counselee invested of himself to become more holy?

c. Has homework been accomplished?
The counselor should ask how motivated the counselee has been to do his homework. In other words, has the counselee done his homework, or has it been a constant struggle for the counselor to get him to complete it due to a lack of understanding and commitment?

5. The helper should consider his self-perspective as he evaluates the counseling process
a. The counselor should ask whether he has tried to work beyond his limitations. In other words, is the helper in a certain counseling situation that is too tough for him to handle?

b. The counselor should ask whether he has tried to maintain a perfectionistic standard. In other words, does the counselor insist that he must succeed with every counselee?
If so, that standard will never be reached, for the counselor is not perfect and no counselee is perfect. Ultimately, the determining factor will be the counselee's willingness to submit to God's lordship and make every effort possible to change the way he thinks and acts.

c. The counselor should ask whether a referral is warranted. In other words, should the counselor refer a counselee to someone else for help?
This becomes an issue when the counselor does not have the expertise or training to handle certain kinds of counseling situations.

d. The counselor should ask whether he is personally walking in fellowship with the Lord

Ineffectiveness in counseling might be due to the helper's poor spiritual vitality and commitment.

e. The counselor should ask whether he needs to consult with his peers

There are times when the counselor should talk with his peers about situations he has encountered.

6. The counselor should evaluate whether he has succeeded or failed in his counseling

a. Success if?

Biblical counseling might be deemed a success if the counselee has learned how to become more Christ-like and how to avoid sinful patterns of behavior in the future (Adams, 1970, p. 57). This statement, of course, makes the goal of counseling the consecration and conversion of the counselee.

b. Failure if?

Biblical counseling might be deemed a failure if the counselee refused to turn to Christ in faith and grow in Christ-likeness. Biblical counselors expect to fail because they are sinners and because the persons they are working with are sinners. Failure is a recognized part of counseling and every counselor who works with others will fail because they are both human.

c. Adams lists several reasons for failure in nouthetic counseling and those same reasons apply to all biblical counselors (see Adams, 1970, pp. 58-59)

1. The counselor might become too sympathetic to the complaints and excuses of the counselee. The counselor has framed the counselee as a victim of his environment, rather than a person responsible for his sinful actions.

2. The counselor might gather an insufficient amount of data and thus come to conclusions too quickly. By failing to gather sufficient data, the counselor is prone to jump to conclusions and make erroneous diagnoses.

3. The counselor might become too emotionally involved in the counselee's problems and thus allow his judgment to be clouded by feelings, rather than reason.

4. The counselor might become overbearing in his use of authority. Rather than being both firm and loving, the counselor comes across in a mean-spirited manner. It is important for biblical counselors to examine their own lives and their counseling practices regularly in the light of every failure they detect in others. Counselees become strong reminders of human error and sin and, in that sense, should keep the biblical counselor sensitive to his own flaws. For this reason counselees are some of the counselor's most valuable teachers.

6. Terminating the counseling relationship

a. How long does biblical counseling take?
Counseling will vary in the amount of time required according to the individual, his motivation, and the particular problem. On the average, biblical counseling requires far less time than conventional secular counseling. One reason is that biblical counselors are not interested in prolonging the number of sessions in order to increase their income. Another reason is that biblical counseling seeks to restore a person to a position of growth in Christ-likeness, not to provide ongoing "therapy" as has become popular in secular models. The biblical counselor will keep in mind that we are all in a growing process and will never arrive at full maturity this side of heaven. We are not looking, therefore, for perfection but for the counselee to acquire the tools to deal with the problem and the demonstration of some consistency over time. We often recommend one month and six month follow-ups for accountability and for any questions that have arisen. In regards to how long the counseling relationship should last the following is offered as a general guideline:

• Simple problems are often solved in one session.

• Severe problems may require a much longer period.

• Marital counseling may require as many as 12 to 18 sessions.

• Substance abuse and pornography problems may require many more sessions, with intensive accountability and follow-up.

• On average we find counseling lasts 8 to 12 sessions with one and six month follow-ups. But it must be stressed that this is only an average.

b. When should the counseling relationship end?
The counseling relationship should end when:
1. The counselee shows he is not willing to work at growth by:
   • excessive absences ...
   • not doing the homework or not working at it seriously ...
   • not putting forth effort toward repentance ...
   • consistently rejecting the advice of the counselor ...
2. When the counselor determines that he does not possess the expertise or experience to best help the counselee.
3. When a crisis in the life of the counselor or counselee makes it necessary to stop.
4. When the counselee has acquired the tools to deal with his problem effectively, has demonstrated growth, and has the commitment to continue to do so.
5. When it becomes clear that the counselee would at this time benefit most from a different kind of relationship such as an accountability group, a Bible study, or a more informal discipleship.

How to end the relationship
As the goals are set in the first sessions it should be clear when those goals have been accomplished. While counselees often resist ending the relationship it should be clear from the beginning that it is the counselor's intention to give the counselee over to his or her shepherding leadership in the local church for continued discipleship.

The counselee should be told that counseling will end a week or two in advance. Many counselors have found it helpful to end the relationship with the giving of a gift. We suggest something like a copy of the devotional book *My Utmost for His Highest* by Oswald Chambers as a daily reminder of God's faithfulness to them in this process and for further growth. It is also appropriate to schedule a follow-up with a clear understanding of the expected growth by that time.

CHAPTER 12

THE WEEKLY COUNSELING RECORD

Introduction

In order for the counselor to discern what is happening from one session to another, he should keep thorough, accurate, and detailed records of what was said and recommended.

1. There is biblical precedent for keeping good counseling records

a. In biblical Christianity

In biblical Christianity, early church leaders recognized the importance of keeping good records. For example, concerning the experience of the Old Testament believers, Paul said in Romans 15:4, "For whatever was written in earlier times was written for our instruction."

b. The Bible itself

The historical books of the Old Testament, the four Gospels, and the book of Acts reflect the work of those who kept accurate, detailed records of what transpired. These documents serve as permanent accounts of what took place in the lives of God's people. They also serve as reminders of His goodness, love, holiness, and judgment (see Romans 10:4).

2. It is wise to keep good counseling records

a. Provides continuity to counseling

Counselors should keep records of each session, to help them to know exactly what is happening in each meeting and in the lives of their counselees.

b. Provides data for interpretation and understanding
Keeping records gives the counselor the data that he needs to isolate the problem, determine the direction, assign homework, and remember the flow of previous appointments.

c. Provides a possible basis for legal protection
In light of the legal climate and the complexities of the judicial system facing counselors, it is best to maintain clear, thorough, and accurate records of each session. It is also wise to speak to a knowledgeable Attorney to be sure he understands the laws related to counseling and record keeping in his area.

3. The content of the weekly counseling record should follow a clear, straightforward, and predictable format (see Adams, 1973, pp. 264, 444 and Appendix 1).[40]
a. Identifying data
At the top of the weekly counseling record should appear some basic but important information, such as the name of the counselee, the case number, the date, the session number, the name of the counselor, and the scheduled date for the next session.

b. Case-numbering system recommended
For legal and confidentiality reasons, some recommend using the case number, not the counselee's name, on the weekly counseling record. A master log of names and case numbers then can be kept locked up in a private storage area, with only designated people having the authority to that master log.

c. Dating gives quick reference to sequencing
The date on the record sheet gives the counselor a quick reference of when he last saw the counselee. The date also serves as a quick identifier of how long the counselor has been seeing the counselee.

---

[40] This weekly record was inspired by the work of Jay Adams and has gone through several revisions.

d. The session number gives quick reference to number of sessions
The session number also can be used to determine how long the counselor has been meeting with the counselee. The session number additionally can indicate the frequency of the meetings.

e. Counselor name helps with administration
The counselor's name appears on the record sheet for secretarial and administrative purposes.

f. Keeping appointments straight
The next session category should contain the agreed upon time the counselor and the counselee plan to meet. It serves as a reminder as well as an accountability check.

4. The counseling record should have a place for reviewing the previous session's homework assignment
a. Evaluating homework is part of the linear and multidimensional process model

b. Reviewing homework space
Having a place set aside on the record sheet for reviewing homework serves as a convenient reminder that this step needs to be done at the beginning of the counseling session. The category on the form also gives the counselor a place to write some detailed and specific information about what the counselee did, how well he did, what his attitude was concerning the assignment, and so forth.

c. Adding additional sheets
On some occasions, it might be necessary for the counselor to attach a separate sheet to the counseling record to report more fully on the counselee's performance of the previous session's homework assignment.

5. The counseling record should have a place for gathering further data
a. Gathering further data is part of the linear and multidimensional process model

b. Value of a format

Having a place set aside for gathering further data serves as a convenient reminder that this step needs to be done during the counseling session. The category on the form also gives the counselor a place to write some detailed and specific information about how the counselee is doing, what problems he faces, what his attitude is regarding his situation, and so forth.

c. Additional pages

On some occasions, it might be necessary for the counselor to attach a separate sheet to the counseling record to give more detailed reporting of the data he gathered during the session.

6. The counseling record should have a place for recording what the counselor discerns the counselee is doing or not doing biblically

a. Discerning data

Discerning what the counselee is doing or not doing biblically helps the counselor to determine the direction and confront the counselee. Thus, this information is key to the linear and multidimensional process models.

b. Definite placement

Having a place set aside for discerning what the counselee is doing or not doing biblically serves as a convenient reminder that this step needs to be done during the counseling session. The category on the form also gives the counselor a place to write some detailed and specific information about what is transpiring in the current session. Additional pages may be added if necessary for recording more detail.

7. The counseling record should have a place for recording the agenda

a. Explore

The agenda includes a category for what needs to be explored in later counseling sessions. This section serves as a reminder of issues raised in the current session that need to be investigated and resolved in subsequent meetings.

b. Hope

The agenda includes a category for giving hope to the counselee for a resolution of his problem. This section serves as a reminder of what the counselor said to reassure the counselee that his problems are solvable and to build up the confidence of the counselee.

c. List

The agenda includes a category for listing problems. This section serves as a reminder of the difficulties facing the counselee that he needs to resolve in a biblical manner. The roster of problems are those that will need to be dealt with from a biblical frame of reference somewhere along the way in the extended counseling process.

d. Assignments

The agenda includes a category for recording the homework assignment the counselor gave to the counselee. This section serves as a reminder of what the counselor asked the counselee to do in preparation for the next session. By spending time with the counselee in this area, the counselor can build into his thinking and understanding God's system of living. The assigning of homework does not need to be left until the end of the session. As a result of any one of the steps in the counseling process – whether it be gathering the data, isolating the counselee's problem, determining the direction the counselee should go, or helping the counselee to rethink his problem – the counselor might think of one or several homework assignments. Making a quick note of these homework ideas during the course of the meeting can serve as a reminder of what the counselor wanted the counselee to do. The notes also can serve as a reminder of how an assignment is logically connected with what was said during the course of the meeting. Even if some of the homework ideas are not used immediately, they might be constructive projects to assign later on in the counseling process.

8. There are several advantages to laying out the agenda (Adams, 1973, p. 230)

a. Encourages return
Laying out the agenda encourages the counselee to return.

b. Encourages realistic view of process
Laying out the agenda encourages the counselee to see that there is much more work to be done.

c. Encourages by projecting a program
Laying out the agenda encourages the counselee to see that the counselor has a plan and program, will move judiciously and measurably through the counseling process, and cares enough to explain what he is doing and why.

Bibliography for Section Three

Adams, Jay E. *A Theology of Christian Counseling: More than Redemption.* Grand Rapids: Zondervan, 1979.

Adams, Jay E. *Competent to Counsel: Introduction to Nouthetic Counseling.* Grand Rapids: Zondervan, 1970.

Adams, Jay E. *The Christian Counselor's Manual: The Practice of Nouthetic Counseling.* Grand Rapids: Zondervan, 1973.

Atkinson, David J., Field, David F., Holmes, Arthur, and O'Donovan, Oliver (eds.). *New Dictionary of Christian Ethics and Pastoral Theology.* Downers Grove, IL: InterVarsity Press, 1995.

Bronner, L. *The Helping Relationship: Process and Skills* Englewood Cliffs, NJ, Prentice Hall, 1973.

Crabb, Larry *Basic Principles of biblical Counseling: Meeting Counseling Needs Through the Local Church.* Grand Rapids: Zondervan, 1975.

Crabb, Larry *Effective Biblical Counseling: A Model for Helping Caring Christians Become Capable Counselors.* Grand Rapids: Zondervan, 1977.

Crabb, Larry *Real Change is Possible – If You're Willing to Start from the Inside Out.* Colorado Springs, CO: NavPress, 1988.

Egan, Gerard *The Skilled Helper: A Systematic Approach to Effective Helping,* Pacific Grove, CA: Brooks/Cole Publishing Co., 1986.

Eyrich, H. A. "Taking Notes in Counseling." In *The Trinity Counselor.* Vol. 1, Issue 1, Fall, 1996.

Hindson, E. and Eyrich, H. *Totally Sufficient* Baker Book House, 1997

Hines, William L. *Leaving Yesterday Behind: A Victim No More.* Tain: Christian Focus, 1997.

Kennedy, Eugene *On Becoming a Counselor: A Basic Guide for non-Professional Counselors,* 1977.

Matzat, Don. "A Better Way: Christ Is My Worth." in *Power Religion: The Selling out of the Evangelical Church?* Michael S. Horton, ed. Chicago: Moody, 1992.

Mowrer, O. Hobart. *The Crisis in Psychiatry and Religion.* Princeton: Van Nostrand Company, 1961.

Powlison, David. "Critiquing Modern Integrationist." In *The Journal of Biblical Counseling.* Vol. XI. No. 3. Spring, 1993.

Powlison, David. "Integration or Inundation?" In *Power Religion: The Selling out of the Evangelical Church?* Michael S. Horton, ed. Chicago: Moody, 1992.

Roberts, Robert C. *Taking the Word to Heart: Self and Other in an Age of Therapies.* Grand Rapids: Eerdmans, 1993)

Welch, Edward. "Codependency and the Cult of the Self." In *Power Religion: The Selling out of the Evangelical Church?* Michael S. Horton, ed. Chicago: Moody, 1992.

Appendix 1

WEEKLY COUNSELING RECORD

Name _____

Date _____

Session # _____

Counselor _____

Next Session _____

Building
Involvement

Evaluate
Homework

Gather
Data

Assign
Homework

Isolate
Problem

Determine
Direction

Gain
Commitment

Rethink
Problem

Give
Hope

Confrontation

1) Review Last Week's Homework	AGENDA To Be Explored Later
2) Gather Further Data	Hope
	Problem List
3) Discern What Counselee is Doing/ Not Doing Biblically	Homework

Appendix 1 (Alternative)

WEEKLY COUNSELING RECORD	

Name _____
Date _____
Session # _____
Counselor _____
Next Session _____

AGENDA:
To Be Explored Later:

Review Last Week's Homework:

Gather Further Data:

Hope:

Problem List:
(isolated problem):

Discern What Counselee is
Doing/ Not Doing Biblically:

Homework:

Appendix 2[41]

PERSONAL DATA INFORMATION FORM

**This form must be completed in full before the first counseling session.
All information is confidential.**

PERSONAL DATA INFORMATION FORM

This form must be completed in full before the first counseling session.
All information is confidential.

IDENTIFICATION DATA

Name_____

Phone_____

Address_____City_____Zip____

Occupaion_____

Phone (H)_____(W)_____

Sex: (M)____(F)____ Birthdate_____ Age_____

Referred here by_____

HEALTH INFORMATION

Rate your health (check): Very Good ____ Good _____ Average____

Declining____ Other_____

Height_____Your approximate weight_____lbs.

Weight changes recently (+/--)_____

List all important present or past illnesses or injuries or handicaps:

_____

Date of last medical examination _____

Report:_____

Your physician _____

Address _____

---

[41] 1. This document was inspired by Jay Adams (see Christian Counselor's Manual), but has been expanded over the years out of our experience and from the suggestions of students.

2. The authors take no legal responsibility for the use of this document. It is strongly recommended that any prospective user check with his/her attorney for liability issues in the state of residence.

Are you presently taking medication: Yes____ No____
What?_____
Have you used drugs for other than medical purposes? Yes__ No____
What?_____
Have you ever been arrested? Yes _____ No _____
Are you willing to sign a release or information form so that your counselor may write for social, psychiatric, or medical reports? Yes ___No___
Have you recently suffered the loss of someone who was close to you? Yes____ No____ last
Explain:

_____

_____

EDUCATION
Education (last year you completed) _____(grade)
Other training (list type and years)

_____

(Include any degrees)

_____

MARRIAGE AND FAMILY INFORMATION
Marital Status: Single____ Going Steady ____ Engaged ____ Married ____
Separated____ Divorced____ Widowed _____
Name of Spouse_____
Address _____-_____
Occupation _____
Phone (H)_____ (W) _____
Your spouse's age_____ Education (in years) _____
Religion_____
spouse willing to come for counseling? Yes ___ No___ Uncertain____
Have you ever been separated? Yes__ No__ When?
from _____to_____
Have either of you ever filed for divorce? Yes___ No___
When _____

Date of marriage _____

Your ages when married: Husband _____ Wife _____

How long did you know your spouse before marriage?_____

Length of steady dating with spouse _____

Length of engagement _____

Give brief information about any previous marriages:

_____

Information about children:

PM* Name   Age   Sex   Living?   Years/   Education   Marital Status

_____

_____

_____

*Check column if child is by previous marriage)

RELIGIOUS BACKGROUND

Denominational preference: _____

Member of_____(church)

How often do you attend per month? (circle) 0 1 2 3 4 5 6 7 8 9 10+

What church did you attend as a child? _____

Baptized?_____

Religious background of spouse (if married) _____

Baptized? _____

Do you consider yourself a religious person? Yes ___ No ___ Uncertain___

Do you believe in God? Yes ___ No ___ Uncertain___

Do you believe Satan exists? Yes ___ No ___ Uncertain___

Have you ever "dabble" with the "Occult"? Yes ___ No ___ Uncertain___

(Seances, devil worship, witchcraft, etc.)

Do you pray to God? Yes __ No____ Never___ Occasionally___ Often___

Would you say you are a Christian? Yes____ No____; or would you

say you are still in the process of becoming a Christian?   _____

How often do you read the Bible? Never___ Occasionally___ Often___

Do you have regular devotions? Yes ___ No___ Not sure what you

mean____ Explain recent changes in your religious life, if any

_____

PERSONALITY INFORMATION:

Have you ever had any psychotherapy or counseling before?
Yes____No_____

If yes, list counselor or therapists and dates:

_____

_____

What was the outcome?

_____

_____

As you see yourself, what kind of person are you? Describe yourself.

What, if anything, do you fear?

Is there any other information that would help us to help you? Have you recently suffered a loss from serious social, business, or other reversals, etc.? Yes____ No___ Explain:

_____

Circle any of the following words which best describe you now:

Godly   Ethical   Hypocritical   Strict   Angry   Unreasonable   Abusive

Irresponsible   Cruel   Uneducated   Proud   Embarrassing   Active

Ambitious   Self-confident   Persistent   Nervous   Hardworking

Impatient   Impulsive   Moody   Often-blue   Excitable   Imaginative

Calm   Serious   Easy-going   Shy   Good-natured   Introvert   Extrovert

Likable   Leader   Quietboiled   Hard-boiled   Submissive   Lonely

Selfconscious   Sensitive   Humorous   Sloppy   Well-groomed

Selfdisciplined   Whiner   Selfish   Lots of Friends   Failure   Success

Other_____

FAMILY AND CHILDHOOD INFORMATION:

If you were reared by anyone other than your own parents, briefly explain:

_____

How many older brothers _____ sisters_____ do you have?

How many younger brothers_____ sisters _____ do you have?

Are   you   on   good   terms   with   your   Mother___

Father____Brother_____Sisters_____?

List the people that you hate or are extremely angry with, and the reasons:

_____

What kind of home did you grow up in? (Check all that apply)

_____ Traditional (Father, Mother, Kids)

_____ Authoritarian (Father or Mother made all the rules without discussion. Would not allow for other opinions.

__ Divorced (Who did you live with? ___Mom ___Dad Other_____)

___ Alcoholic (___Skid row ___Functional, but affected ___Dysfunctional effect on family)

__Drug Affected (__Cocaine__Heroin__Marijuana ___Other_____)

_____ Perfectionist (Everything had to be done just right to please ___Mom ____Dad____Both

_____ Critical (One or both parents could only remark about the negatives. Little praise for good things).

_____ Affectionate (___Demonstrative with hugs, kisses, etc. ___Affection there, but not openly shown).

_____ Emotional (___Crying allowed, but controlled. ___Anger, screaming freely allowed).

_____ Repressed (__Emotions not allowed to show. ___Parents showed emotion, but kids not allowed to do so).

_____ Religious (__In name only ___Strict, negative ___ Hypocritical ___Genuine Happy Experience).

_____ Step-family (___Which of parents remarried? _____ ___ Had to live with step-brothers or step-sisters)

_____ Abusive (In what way? ___ Sexual ___Physical Beatings ___Emotional ___ Other: _____)

FAMILY AND CHILDHOOD INFORMATION CONTINUED:

What kind of home did your Father grow up in?____ Traditional (Father, Mother, Kids)

_____ Authoritarian (Father or Mother made all the rules without discussion.

_____ Would not allow for other opinions.

____ Divorced (Who did you live with? ___Mom ___Dad Other_____)

____ Alcoholic (___Skid row ___Functional, but affected ___Dysfunctional effect on family)

____ Drug Affected (___Cocaine ___Heroin ___Marijuana ___ Other_____)

____ Perfectionist (Everything had to be done just right to please ___Mom ___Dad____Both

____ Critical (One or both parents could only remark about the negatives. Little praise for good things).

____ Affectionate (___Demonstrative with hugs, kisses, etc. ___Affection there, but not openly shown).

____ Emotional (___Crying allowed, but controlled. ___Anger, screaming freely allowed).

____ Repressed (__Emotions not allowed to show. ___Parents showed emotion, but kids not allowed to do so).

____ Religious (__In name only ___Strict, negative __ Hypocritical ___Genuine Happy Experience).

____ Step-family (___Which of parents remarried? _____ ___ Had to live with step-brothers or step-sisters)

____ Abusive (In what way? ___ Sexual ___Physical Beatings ___Emotional ___Other: _____)

What kind of home did your Mother grow up in? ____ Traditional (Father, Mother, Kids) ____ Authoritarian (Father or Mother made all the rules without discussion. Would not allow for other opinions.

___Divorced (Who did you live with? __Mom __Dad Other_____)

_____ Alcoholic (___Skid row ___Functional, but affected

___Dysfunctional effect on family)

_____ Drug Affected (___Cocaine ___Heroin ___Marijuana ____ Other_____)

_____ Perfectionist (Everything had to be done just right to please ___Mom ___Dad___Both

_____ Critical (One or both parents could only remark about the negatives. Little praise for good things).

_____ Affectionate (___Demonstrative with hugs, kisses, etc. ___Affection there, but not openly shown).

_____ Emotional (___Crying allowed, but controlled. ___Anger, screaming freely allowed).

_____ Repressed (___Emotions not allowed to show. ___Parents showed emotion, but kids not allowed to do so).

_____ Religious (___In name only ___Strict, negative ____ Hypocritical ___Genuine Happy Experience).

_____ Step-family (___Which of parents remarried? _____

____ Had to live with step-brothers or step-sisters)

_____ Abusive (In what way? ____ Sexual ___Physical Beatings ___Emotional ____ Other: _____)

FAMILY AND CHILDHOOD INFORMATION CONTINUED

Would you characterize your Father as: (Circle the appropriate words)

Godly   Ethical   Hypocritical   Strict   Angry   Unreasonable   Abusive

Irresponsible   Cruel   Uneducated   Proud   Embarrassing   Active

Ambitious   Self-confident   Persistent   Nervous   Hardworking

Impatient   Impulsive   Moody   Often-blue   Excitable   Imaginative

Calm   Serious   Easy-going   Shy   Good-natured   Introvert   Extrovert

Likable   Leader   Quietboiled   Hard-boiled   Submissive   Lonely

Selfconscious   Sensitive   Humorous   Sloppy   Well-groomed

Selfdisciplined   Whiner   Selfish   Lots of Friends   Failure   Success

Other_____

Would you characterize your Mother as:

Godly Ethical Hypocritical Strict Angry Unreasonable Abusive
Irresponsible Cruel Uneducated Proud Embarrassing Active
Ambitious Self-confident Persistent Nervous Hardworking
Impatient Impulsive Moody Often-blue Excitable Imaginative
Calm Serious Easy-going Shy Good-natured Introvert Extrovert
Likable Leader Quietboiled Hard-boiled Submissive Lonely
Selfconscious Sensitive Humorous Sloppy Well-groomed
Selfdisciplined Whiner Selfish Lots of Friends Failure Success
Other_____

Where did you grow up? ___Urban Area ___Suburban Area _____ Small
Town _____Rural _____Farm City, State _____
Population_____
What was your family's economic situation when you were a child?
_____ Extremely poor ____Poor ____Lower Middle Income _____ Middle
Income _____ Higher Middle Income ____Wealthy _____ Extremely wealthy
Where you ever sexually abused by anyone? ____No ____Yes
(Please detail: ___Were you abused by a relative? ____Were you abused
by a stranger? _____A neighbor? How old were you at the time?_____
Was the person who abused you ever prosecuted?_____
What was your happiest memory as a child?_____
_____

What was your unhappiest memory as a child?
_____
_____

Did you experience a major trauma when you were a child? Detail:
_____ At Home
_____

_____ At School
_____

____ At Neighbor's Home_____

____ At Relative's Home_____

____ Other: _____

TELEVISION & ENTERTAINMENT

How much television do you watch each day?_____hrs.

List your favoriteprograms:_____

What is your favorite type of music?_____

List your favorite entertainers:

_____

BIO-PSYCHOLOGICAL INFORMATION

Have you ever felt people were watching you? Yes_____ No_____

Do people's faces ever seem distorted? Yes_____ No_____

Do you ever have difficulty distinguishing faces? Yes _____ No_____

Do colors ever seem too bright? Yes _____ No_____

Are you sometimes unable to judge distance? Yes _____ No_____

Have you ever had hallucinations? Yes _____ No_____

Are you afraid of being in a car? Yes _____ No_____

Is your hearing exceptionally good? Yes _____ No_____

Do you have problems sleeping? Yes _____ No_____

PERSONAL BEHAVIORAL HABITS

1. Do you drink coffee or other caffeinated drinks? Yes ____ No____ How much per day?_____.

2. Do you smoke? Yes_____ No_____ How much?_____.

3. Do you explode when you get angry? Yes_____ No _____.

4. Do you withdraw when you get angry or hurt? Yes_____ No_____.

5. Do you frequently argue with significant other people? Yes___No_____

WOMEN ONLY

Have you had any menstrual difficulties?_____

Do you experience tension, tendency to cry, other symptoms prior to your cycle? Please explain:

_____

Is your husband willing to come for counseling?

Is he in favor of your coming ? _____ If no, explain

_____

BRIEFLY ANSWER THE FOLLOWING QUESTIONS
1. What is your problem?

2. What have you done about it?

3. What can we do? (What are your expectations in coming here?)

4. Is there any other information we should know?

PROBLEM CHECK LIST: (Check those which are current)
_____ Anger _____ Envy _____ Appetite
_____ Anxiety _____ Fear _____ Memory
_____ Apathy _____ Gluttony _____ Moodiness
_____ Bitterness _____ Guilt _____ Rebellion
_____ Change in Lifestyle _____ Health _____ Sex
_____ Children _____ Homosexuality _____ Sleep
_____ Depression _____ Impotence _____ Wife Abuse
_____ Deception _____ In-laws _____ A Vice

COUNSELING INFORMATION AND CONTRACT

1. Diagnostic Tools: We use helpful counseling forms such as this Personal Data Information form, the Problem Pattern Analysis form, and other aids to gain an understanding of the central problems a person is experiencing.

2. Intent Listening: We encourage the counselee to speak his mind in an appropriate fashion and to discuss his thoughts, anxieties, resentments, and fears so that the counselor will have a clear understanding of the central problems.

3. Team Counseling: There are times when a counseling situation may call for a team approach. In this event, we may have more than one counselor involved in a session. The counselors share insights and opinions with one another which pertain to the case. Team Counseling can be especially helpful in marital counseling; a husband and wife team can help put both counselees at ease.

4. Assignments: Counselees make more rapid progress when they are required to study or to perform specific informational or behavioral assignments which pertain to the problem. We tailor these assignments to the individual counselee and the circumstances.

5. Accountability: We are not interested in wasting the time of the counselors or the counselees. We are interested in believers learning how to experience the peace and joy that result from a walk of obedience to God's Word, and we hold the counselees accountable for doing the assignments on schedule.

How long does biblical counseling take?
Counseling will vary in the amount of time required according to the individual, his motivation, and the particular problem. On the average, however, biblical counseling requires far less time than conventional secular counseling. One reason is that biblical counselors are not interested in prolonging the number of sessions in order to increase their income. Simple problems

are often solved in one session. Severe problems may require a longer period. Marital counseling may require as many as 12 to 18 sessions. Substance abuse problems may require many more sessions, with intensive accountability and follow-up.

How much does it cost?
The counselor will discuss this with the counselee.

About confidentiality
We are careful to protect each counselee's confidentiality. There are times, however, when a counselor must consult with other counselors for advice. If information is revealed in counseling which indicates a genuine potential for harm to a counselee or others, the counselor may be required by law or biblical mandate to share that information with the appropriate authorities or family members.

COUNSELING CONTRACT

I, (name) _____, affirm the accuracy of the personal information provided herein, and have read the information above and agree to the conditions set forth therein. I hereby agree to the following conditions:

1. I am committed to changing my life by coming into obedience to the Word of God.
2. I will keep the appointment time, or will call to cancel in advance with a legitimate reason.
3. I will fulfill the weekly assignments.
4. I will attend church each Sunday while I am in counseling.
5. I understand that confidentiality cannot be guaranteed in the case of information as indicated above.

(Signed)_____(Date)_____

Appendix 3

Four Levels of Problems and their Solutions

Downward Spiral   Upward Spiral

Perception Level: Where the Problem Begins
Mind-set, belief, established attitude
interpretation of reality, idols of the heart

Preconditioning Level
Learn patterns, chronic anger, avoidance
of conflict, lying, self-pity, deceit,
immorality, self-orientated fulfillment.

Performance Level
This is the "doing level." Ask what,
when, how and who questions to discover
"why" this behavior is characteristic of the
counselee.

Performance includes: brooding, slander,
perversion, short-tempered, overeating,
slamming doors, holding grudges, critical,
clamming up, etc.

Developing Spiritual Dimensions

Presences level
What is felt: This includes what a person
projects – constant frown, rigid muscle tone
– and what he feels and talks about feeling.
Severely depressed, listless, confused, fearful,
drug dependent, poor interpersonal
relationships, unable to control anger, suicidal.

Grateful acknowledgement is made to Jay E. Adams for the basic
ideas presented here. Some information has been added by the
authors.

Scripture Index

4:23 18
4:24 46
4:25 46
4:26 46
4:27 46, 47
6:21 46
7:3 46
11:20 46
13:12 153
14:14 46
15:15 46, 47
15:23 44
15:30 46, 47
18:13 100
18:15 100
18:17 100
19:19 111
22:19 41
22:20 41
23:7 122
25:21-22 125
28:14 47
30:5 22
30:5-6 22, 28
30:6 22

Ecclesiastes
12:1-8 139
12:13-14 145

Isaiah
1:16-17 114
6:8 150
6:10 45
40:8 23
55:11 30
59:2 121
63:10 61

Jeremiah
13:23 112
15:16 73
17:9 21
23:29 41
30:2 22, 41
45:1-2 41

Lamentations
3:19-24 140

Ezekiel
2:7 22
36:25-28 48

Daniel
4:34-35 20, 22

Habakkuk
2:2 41

Zechariah
9:9 73

Matthew
4 31
4:1 61
5:3 72
5:4 72
5:5 72
5:6 73
5:8 45, 52, 73
5:9 74
5:10 74
5:17 23
5:17-19 39
5:20 71
6:33 78
7:24 146
7:24-29 50

7:48-50 146
10:26-31 20
10:28 20
11:28-30 146
11:29 73
12:31 61
12:34 18, 45
12:34-35 122
15:1-3 41
18:21-35 73
22:37 45
23:25-28 74
24:35 23
28:20 146

Mark
7:7-13 41
7:20-23 46
10:45 119
12:29-32 58
13:31 39

Luke
4:14 61
4:16-21 72
6:22-23 74
6:26 74
6:45 18
10:25-37 76
10:30-37 73
12:4-5 51
12:12 61
14:31-33 72
15:11-32 72
17:3 74
24:17-21 44
24:25 22
24:44 41

Subject Index

Biographical Information for Howard A. Eyrich, D.Min.
Howard's career includes planting a church in Eastern Pennsylvania, founding the Center for Biblical Counseling and Education in St. Louis, Missouri, serving on the faculties of Covenant Theological Seminary, Trinity Bible College and Theological Seminary and Birmingham Theological Seminary. He is the author of *Three To Get Ready: A Premarital Counseling Manual* and *The Christian Handbook on Aging* as well as co-author/editor of *Totally Sufficient* and *Homework CD for Biblical Counseling, Vol. 1* with Bill Hines. He currently serves Briarwood Presbyterian Church in Birmingham, Alabama, as an Associate Pastor with pastoral responsibility for two congregational communities, theological education, and counseling.

Biographical Information for William L. Hines, D.Min.

Bill Hines (B.A. Political Science; M.A. Counseling; M.A. Religion; D.Min. Counseling) is the President of Covenant Ministries, Inc., a biblical counseling and education ministry in Ft. Worth, Texas. Author of *Leaving Yesterday Behind: A Victim No More; Homework CD for Biblical Counseling, Vol. 1 (with Howard Eyrich)*. Bill has written numerous articles on the Christian life including a monthly column in *Pressing On,* a publication of Covenant Ministries, Inc. A frequent speaker on topics concerning counseling and the Christian life, Bill conducts seminars and training around the US and abroad. Bill serves as adjunct faculty for LeTourneau University and Trinity Bible College and Seminary.

An ordained minister since 1985, Bill is a Mentor and Board Member for the International Association of Biblical Counselors and a certified member of the National Association of Nouthetic Counselors.

Bill and his wife, Kathy, have four daughters and one son and reside in Ft. Worth, Texas.